THE
St Kilda Steamers
A History of McCallum, Orme & Co.

THE
St Kilda Steamers
A HISTORY OF McCALLUM, ORME & CO.

JAMES MACKAY

TEMPUS

First published 2006

Tempus Publishing Limited
The Mill, Brimscombe Port,
Stroud, Gloucestershire, GL5 2QG
www.tempus-publishing.com

British Library Cataloguing in Publication Data.
A catalogue record for this book is available from the British Library.

ISBN 0 7524 3878 6

Typesetting and origination by Tempus Publishing Limited
Printed in Great Britain

Contents

For Selena,
whose grandparents first met on St Kilda

Preface

My interest (which has become a life-long passion) in the remote island of St Kilda began in March 1959 when, as a young Army officer, I was posted to the Rocket Range in the Outer Hebrides and was immediately sent out to the island aboard the trawler *Mull*, a former Isles Class ship of 575 tons operated by the Royal Army Service Corps, or rather a civilian crew hired by the Ministry of Defence for that purpose. The helmsman, who I remember only as Ould Paddy, was a veritable 'Ancient Mariner' who claimed to have first gone to sea in the days of sail. More importantly, however, he had been a deck-hand on the *Dunara Castle*, the steamer which had served St Kilda so well between 1877 and 1939. He was thus a link with a vanished way of life which, by the 1950s, seemed like ancient history.

Over the next two and a half years I visited St Kilda many times and spent a total of 290 days on the island, latterly as Relief Officer commanding the tiny military garrison. During this period I was lucky enough to contact many of the surviving St Kildans, notably Alexander Gillies Ferguson, one of the most remarkable men I have ever met and who surely deserves a biography. He often regaled me with fascinating anecdotes about his boyhood back in the 1880s. Once I asked him why he had never written a book about St Kilda, but he smiled cryptically and said: 'They would never have forgiven me for that.' It is a strange fact that no native of St Kilda ever produced a book about his or her island, which, considering the enormous literature on the subject, is quite amazing.

St Kilda can only be described in superlatives: the most remote of the British Isles, possessing the highest cliffs and the largest colonies of puffins, gannets and fulmars. The ruins of its ancient village, abandoned in August 1930, were almost obliterated in 1957 when the Ministry of Defence took it over as a missile-tracking station for the Rocket Range and proposed to use the rubble of the buildings to create a road. Fortunately, St Kilda had just been bequeathed by the Marquess of Bute to the National Trust for Scotland who leased it to the Nature Conservancy and these two organisations successfully did battle with the bureaucrats of Whitehall. No one realised at the time what a national treasure was nearly lost. Today, St Kilda is virtually unique in enjoying triple UNESCO World Heritage status as a natural, maritime and cultural site.

Millions of words have been written about St Kilda, dealing largely with its unique wildlife, from the distinctive St Kilda fieldmouse and house mouse to the Soay sheep and the St Kilda wren, not to mention the aquatic mammals and the birdlife in general. Much less has been written about the human population and remarkably little about the steamships which provided a tenuous link between the island and the outside world. In my time we were grateful (perhaps not nearly grateful enough) for the communications provided by the *Mull* in the long winter months and the LCTs (Landing Craft Tanks) which provisioned us in the all too brief summer periods. But we also relied initially on the Fleetwood trawlers, many of which had been afloat when the St Kildans relied on them too.

The core of this book chronicles the development of the regular communications provided by the ships of two Glasgow-based companies, operated by John McCallum and Martin Orme, which amalgamated in 1929 and continued to serve St Kilda not only at the time of the evacuation in August 1930 but in the years when the 'desert isle' acquired a new attraction for the hardiest tourists, up until the outbreak of the Second World War in September 1939.

The exploits of the little coastal steamers, the *Lady Ambrosine*, *Hebridean* and *Hebrides* of John McCallum and the redoubtable *Dunara Castle* of Martin Orme, are placed in their context, which begins with the *Glen Albyn* of 1834 and the *Vulcan* of 1838, the first (and for many years the only) excursion steamers, followed by the steam yachts of wealthy businessmen and landowners. Along the way I record the input of the Royal Navy from Captain Otter in the 1850s, to the patrol ships of the First World War and, fittingly, the role of HMS *Harebell* in the evacuation of the islanders in 1930. Neither the fishing trawlers of Fleetwood and Aberdeen, nor the Norwegian whalers of the early twentieth century, are forgotten. Even in my day (1959–61) we often had cause to be grateful to the Spanish trawlers from Bilbao and Santander and the Breton crabbers from Finistere and Concarneau. My own experience was confirmed by Alexander

Gillies Ferguson who told me that, far from being isolated from the outside world, it often seemed that the island was at the very centre of it, with far more contact with Europe than most places in mainland Britain.

This book not only sets out to chronicle an aspect of transport history associated with one particular remote island, but also to shed new light on the relationship between the people who lived there and the people who fleetingly visited them.

James Mackay
Glasgow
April 2006

One

Earliest
Steamers

Steam navigation in the waters off the west coast of Scotland made enormous strides in the early nineteenth century. Barely seven years after Henry Bell's *Comet* began plying between Greenock and Helensburgh in the sheltered waters of the Firth of Clyde the first steamboats were venturing as far south as Campbeltown. In 1819 a paddle steamer successfully rounded the dangerous Mull of Kintyre, but most coastal vessels preferred to take the short-cut through the Crinan Canal (opened in 1795) to reach Oban. An t-Oban Lathurnaich (literally 'the little inlet of Lorne') rapidly developed as the principal port for the West Highlands and the springboard to the islands of the Inner Hebrides. Eventually it would be connected to Glasgow and other towns and cities by road and rail, but in the early nineteenth century it depended largely on coastal shipping for its communications.

Further north, communications between the mainland of the Highlands and Skye, and thence to the Outer Hebrides, were much slower to develop. Poolewe in Wester Ross was the traditional port for sailing smacks bound for Stornoway (Lewis) or Tarbert (Harris), while virtually the only link between the Uists and the mainland was via Dunvegan on the north-west coast of Skye. From Dunvegan (a village of some importance as the seat of the MacLeods of Harris and Skye) a road ran south via Sligachan and Sconser to Broadford and beyond. Nowadays one can cross from the mainland at Kyle of Lochalsh to Kyleakin in Skye by a handsome bridge. Kyle, as a seaport, dates only from the end of the nineteenth century when the railway from Inverness via Dingwall was completed. Prior to that time, the steamer from Portree sailed to Strome Ferry. Similarly the fishing port of Mallaig, which provided the steamship connection with Armadale in the Sleat peninsula of Skye, only developed on the completion of the railway from Fort William, also in the 1890s.

Consequently, the traditional method of reaching destinations in the Outer Hebrides was by the coastal steamers from Glasgow and Greenock which served the ports, large and small, of the west coast. By the 1840s several companies, usually owners of a single steamship, were serving this route, carrying mainly freight, but also passengers. The round trip from Greenock to the Western Isles took ten days on average, so it was a leisurely voyage, with frequent stops at little fishing villages. If you had business in the islands you would not have to be in a hurry to get there.

The first steamer to visit St Kilda was the *Glen Albyn*. Named after a beauty spot near Stillorgan in County Dublin, she was built in 1834 for the Glen Albyn Steamboat Co., a consortium of landowners and merchants in the West Highlands and Islands, managed on their behalf by Alexander McEachern of Tobermory and based at Crinan or Oban. She made twice-weekly trips to Mull, with excursions to Iona and Staffa, and occasionally sailed to Skye and the Outer Isles until 1837 when she was sold to the North British Steam Navigation Co., part of the group owned by the brothers George and James Burns. With a gross tonnage of 131 and a length of 121ft, she was the largest steamship plying to the Hebrides at that time. She made her maiden voyage from Glasgow on 21 July 1834 under the command of Daniel Matheson. Contemporary newspaper advertisements describe her as 'elegantly furnished'. She sailed down the Firth of Clyde, round the Mull of Kintyre and headed for Oban, where more passengers boarded, circumnavigated the island of Mull, with a brief pilgrimage at Iona and a visit to Fingal's Cave, Staffa, before returning to Oban. Thence she journeyed to and from Inverness via the Caledonian Canal.

By 25 July she was back at Oban. It seems clear that most of her passengers were day trippers, but on this occasion several people came aboard with the intention of visiting an island of which many had heard but which very few had ever seen – St Kilda. The following day the *Glen Albyn* left Tobermory and rounded Ardnamurchan, the most westerly point of the British mainland, and sailed north to Skye. After excursions to the celebrated Spar Cave and Loch Appin, the ship called in at Loch Bracadale on the west coast of Skye, where the passengers were joined by a team of geologists including Jameson Torrie, whose letter to his mother in Edinburgh a week later provided the only eyewitness account of the epic voyage to the farthest Hebrides. According to Torrie, the ship was carrying about sixty passengers, mostly from Glasgow or Inverness but including 'a few young Englishmen and foreigners'.

The ship berthed at Loch Bracadale early on Sunday, a day behind schedule, and immediately set sail for St Kilda, via the Sound of Harris. She arrived at her ultimate destination shortly before midnight 'but did not venture to anchor that night as there was no one on board who was acquainted with the landing place'. Dawn broke around 4 a.m. on Monday and, at last, the tiny vessel ventured into Village Bay and dropped anchor. Understandably, at that early hour there was no sigh of life, so Captain Matheson ordered that the ship's two cannons be fired to rouse the inhabitants. 'The excitement and astonishment produced by our appearance were great', wrote Torrie.

According to one account, the noise of gunfire and the sight of a strange ship belching smoke from her funnel terrified the islanders, who abandoned their houses and fled for shelter in a deep gully. Although there is no reference to St Kilda ever having been attacked by Barbary pirates, the predations of these seaborne gangsters as far north as the Faroes were doubtless well-known, even in remote St Kilda.

Torrie's account does not confirm this natural reaction and he merely goes on to state that 'we were soon surrounded by the whole population amounting at this time to 93 persons… The clergyman [the Rev. Neil Mackenzie] showed us the lions of the place, and the people were most anxious to show us every thing they thought could interest us and equally so to see the wonders of the vessel, more especially the ornaments and mirrors of the cabin'. Another, but anonymous, account states that shortly before the ship weighed anchor several of the St Kilda men came aboard to look with amazement on the ship's fittings and machinery.

A transcript of one tourist's comments on this visit was published in the *Glasgow Free Press* of 2 August 1834 and gave a hint of mainland attitudes over the intervening years when the St Kildans became an object of interest to Victorian travellers:

At length the party took leave of that simple-minded and warm-hearted little community, with feelings of deep interest and commiseration, hoping that the visit might be remembered in their annals as the commencing point in the era of improvement. Yet they could not altogether suppress their fears, that if a visit to St Kilda should become a common occurrence in parties of pleasure, it might unfortunately happen, that the vices of civilised life would be imparted to them sooner than its virtues and its blessings.

Soon afterwards St Kilda was visited by another steamer, the *Lady of St Kilda*. This was a two-masted schooner which had only recently been converted to steam and was on her maiden voyage. This ship was named by her owner, Sir Thomas Dyke Acland, in honour of his wife Lydia, who had previously accompanied him on a visit in his private yacht in 1812 and was apparently the first female to visit St Kilda. Sir Thomas was a wealthy baronet from Devon with commercial and shipping interests. The maiden voyage of his steamship was, in fact, a complete circumnavigation of the British mainland, with visits to the offshore islands. The climax of the voyage was, of course, an excursion to the island whose name the ship bore.

Like so many other visitors to St Kilda in the eighteenth and early nineteenth centuries, Acland was appalled at the squalor and wretchedness of the cluster of hovels which someone once compared unfavourably to a Hottentot kraal. Acland, however, was one of the few visitors who were prepared to do something to ameliorate conditions. On this occasion he and Lady Lydia not only distributed the customary gifts of tobacco and confectionery but also more practical presents of linens and flannels, enough to provide the women with two shifts apiece in order to encourage them to wash their underclothing more often. Sir Thomas also left £20 with the minister, to be awarded to the first man who rebuilt his house. Mackenzie shrewdly put the money towards an ambitious scheme to create an entirely new village in a crescent above the bay, and thus the so-called '1830s houses' were initiated by the generosity of an English baronet.

The *Lady of St Kilda* was a much larger vessel than the *Glen Albyn*, with excellent accommodation and furnished in the height of luxury. On this occasion a party of women from the island was invited aboard, to be entertained by Lady Lydia on her pianoforte, 'and her family, joining her in a charming chorus, showed them the power of music', as it was described in a vivid account in the *Inverness Courier* of 17 June 1835.

For such a prestigious voyage, Sir Thomas had secured the services of Captain Fairfax Moresby, RN. Born in 1786, he had entered the Royal Navy as an able seaman in 1799, when the Napoleonic Wars were at their height, and progressed through the ranks, becoming a master's mate in the year of Trafalgar. He was commissioned in 1806, promoted to commander in 1811, and to captain in 1814. He stayed at that rank for thirty-five years before his promotion to rear admiral. Thereafter, he advanced to vice admiral in 1856 and admiral in 1862. Appointed a Companion of the Bath in 1815, he was knighted in 1855 and ended up as a Knight Grand Cross of the Bath (GCB) in 1865, dying in 1877 at the age of ninety-one. For many years after the conclusion of the Napoleonic Wars, however, he was 'on the beach', presumably eking out his half pay with whatever maritime commissions came his way, hence his employment by Acland. Port Moresby, the capital city of Papua New Guinea, was named in his honour by his son, Captain John Moresby, who first surveyed the coast in 1873.

There are other connections with the South Pacific. By 1840 the *Lady of St Kilda* was being used by Sir Thomas as a cargo vessel operating between England and Australia and, late the following year, she came to rest in Port Phillip Bay, a few miles south-east of Melbourne, Victoria. Here he offered her for sale or exchange and apparently a local businessman, J.B. Were, acquired an interest in her. It is from this ship that the city of St Kilda, founded in 1842, took its name, one of its principal thoroughfares bearing the name of Acland Street to this day.

The construction of the twenty-one houses forming the new village, begun in the summer of 1835, was not completed by the summer of 1838 when St Kilda was next visited by a steamship. The paddle steamer *Vulcan* was the second Clyde-built ship of that name, superseding the first iron-hulled vessel of 1819, which had served as a passage boat on the Forth and Clyde Canal, and deserves her place in maritime history for revolutionising shipbuilding and helping to make the Clyde the world leader in marine engineering and naval architecture.

This second *Vulcan*, however, was a wooden ship, built by John Wood of Port Glasgow in 1833. She was 141ft long, 22ft 10in in the beam and had a depth of 15ft, with a gross tonnage of 214 (although advertisements exaggerated this and claimed that she was 'of 300 tons burthen'). She was a paddle steamer and her engine was constructed by Robert Napier. She was registered at Glasgow by the City of Glasgow Steam Packet Co., which operated her on the route between Glasgow and Liverpool. The company, formed in 1831, included among its partners the celebrated marine engineer Robert Napier and James Thomson, senior partner in the firm of steamboat agents, Thomson & MacConnell of Glasgow. From being merely agents, Thomson & MacConnell expanded into the operation of their own fleet from April 1838, when they acquired the wooden paddle steamer *Tobermory*, built two years earlier. The Thomson & MacConnell fleet was taken over in 1844 by the City of Glasgow Steam Packet Co. Rather confusingly, this was a new company, the original company of that name having been taken over by George and James Burns in 1840. In turn, their partnership evolved into the Clyde Steam Navigation Co., of whom Thomson & MacConnell continued as Glasgow agents until 1850. There was an extraordinary web of relationships and partnerships in the various concerns associated with shipping in the west of Scotland in this early formative period.

The paddle steamer *Vulcan*, which made one of the earliest excursions to St Kilda, in 1838.

Advertisements and shipping notices in the *Glasgow Herald* indicate that she sailed between the Clyde and Liverpool every four or five days on average, under the command of Captain Colin Ferguson, alternating with the steamers *City of Glasgow* and *Commodore* of the same company.

In 1839 the Western Club of Glasgow chartered the vessel to convey them to Ayr for the famous Eglinton Tournament. During 1840, however, the ship was sold to foreigners and nothing is known of her subsequent career. She may (or may not) have been the 'old steamship' of that name, wrecked on the Vows Rocks off Elie in 1882.

By 1838 the chairman of the City of Glasgow Steam Packet Co. was Archibald MacConnell, a partner in the firm of 'steamboat agents' of Thomson & MacConnell, who organised the trip to St Kilda and was in overall command of the expedition. The advertisement for the 'Pleasure Excursion' appeared in the *Glasgow Herald* on Monday 16 July 1838, and was repeated on Friday 20 July and Monday 23 July. It appears to have been the first cruise of this type ever advertised in a Scottish newspaper.

PLEASURE EXCURSION TO ST. KILDA,
GIANTS' CAUSEWAY, STAFFA, IONA, COULIN
HILLS, AND SPAR CAVE, IN SKYE.

IT is intended that the Splendid, Powerful
and Swift-sailing Steamer VULCAN,
500 Tons Burthen, Captain Colin Ferguson,
will Sail from GLASGOW at 2 P.M., on Wednesday the 25th July, for the above-mentioned places.

The Route proposed is as follows:—
To proceed from GLASGOW to the GIANTS' CAUSE-
WAY on the North Coast of Ireland, allowing Passengers
time to Land and examine its Caves and Basaltic Columns;
from which she will Sail on Thursday Morning, by the
runs of Islay, calling at the celebrated Islands of Iona and
Staffa, (allowing Passengers sufficient time to land and view
these places) to Tobermory in the Sound of Mull, where she
will arrive that evening. She will sail from thence on Friday
morning, by the Islands of Egg and Rum, to the Spar Cave
and the magnificent Coolin Hills in Skye; after visiting
which, she will sail along the south coast of the Isle of Skye
to Lochmaddy in North Uist, where she will arrive that night.
On Saturday morning she will proceed direct from thence to
the Sound of Harris

TO ST. KILDA;
where she will remain till Monday Morning, thereby allowing
Passengers abundance of time to land and survey that interesting Island,—returning from thence by the Sound of Harris
to Lochmaddy, round the north coast of Skye, calling at
Portree, and through the Inner Sounds to Tobermory and
Oban, and back to Glasgow, where it is expected she will
arrive on Wednesday.

Such is the Route proposed, subject to such variations as the
state of the weather may render necessary, Passengers will
have an opportunity of surveying, and all in the space of one
week, not only whatever is interesting and splendid in the
Scenery of the Western Hebrides of Scotland, and the Highlands and bold Coast of the County of Antrim in Ireland,
but of minutely examining the Basaltic Columns and Caves of
Staffa and the Giants' Causeway, together with the Ruins of
the Ancient Monastery of Iona, and that hitherto almost unknown and unvisited Island of St. Kilda. It may be safely
affirmed, that it is quite impossible for strangers by any other
means in the same space of time, and at so small an expense
to visit so much of the splendid scenery of Scotland and
Ireland.

Fares, £5 for the round, wherever taken on Board.
Breakfast, Dinner, Tea and Supper, will be provided by
the Stewards at 5s. per day, for each Passenger for each day
he may be on Board. Wines and Liquors at the usual prices.
As it is intended to issue only Sixty Tickets, an early application will be necessary, for no one can be taken on board
for the round who has not previously taken out a Ticket, with
the number of the berth thereby secured.
Plans of the Cabin may be seen by applying to Messrs.
M'Iver & Co., Liverpool; Kippen & Lindsay, Greenock; Hall
Charley, Belfast. Berths only secured at the Office, 15, Jamaica Street, Glasgow.

THOMSON & MACCONNELL.

An advertisement for *Vulcan's* cruise to St Kilda, published in the *Glasgow Herald*, 1838.

On this occasion Colin Ferguson (although advertised as the skipper) handed over command of the ship to Captain James McKillop, normally in charge of her sister ship, the *Toward Castle*, which was employed on the Glasgow–Belfast route. It may well be that McKillop was selected for this experiment because he was very familiar with the coast of Northern Ireland, the first port of call. The cost of the excursion – £5 for seven days, plus 5s a day for meals (a total of £6 15s) – would be equivalent to about £1,200 today.

Lachlan MacLean, who published an account of the voyage, gives the names of about thirty passengers. This was about half the number hoped for, and this may explain why the experiment was not repeated. As well as the thirty passengers, the *Vulcan* had on board a brass band, which played fortissimo as the ship entered Village Bay. The noise, and the smoke and fire belching from her funnel, terrified the St Kildans, who fled to the hills, just as they had done four years earlier.

The advertisements which appeared in the newspaper indicate that St Kilda was the chief attraction. Not only was the notice boldly headed 'PLEASURE EXCURSION TO ST KILDA', but the name of the island was repeated in bold capitals halfway down the tightly packed text.

The ship left the Broomielaw in Glasgow at 2.30 p.m. on Wednesday 25 July and journeyed first to the Giant's Causeway, then north to Fingal's Cave at Staffa, followed by Eigg and Rum, and on to the Spar Cave, Fingal's Nursery and Loch Scavaig in Skye. She crossed the Minch to Lochmaddy, where several of the party took the opportunity to go aboard the immigrant ship *Corsair*, which was about to depart from North Uist with a large number of islanders bound for Cape Breton and the uncertainties of a new life in Nova Scotia. Describing this 'heart-rending scene' MacLean lamented 'the idea of so many fine fellows and fine women being decoyed to Cape Breton – the very St Kilda of America!' While other passengers retired for the night the indefatigable MacLean went ashore to visit the local inn. After several mishaps and escapades, he finally reached his goal around midnight on Friday where the local gentry were having a late-night carouse. Lachlan was particularly intrigued by the barman, 'a black fellow who spoke and sang Gaelic!'

Although MacLean seems to have spent half the night at the revels, he was awake in time to witness the ship get under way at 5 a.m. on Saturday. He then 'steered the tortuosity' of the Sound of Harris, from which they got their first glimpse of St Kilda on the far horizon. They reached their destination about 10 a.m. and sailed round Boreray and the Stacks, loosing off the ship's cannon and taking pot-shots at the gannets with their rifles. So loud was the detonation of the ship's most powerful cannon that MacLean, who was standing close-by as the ship nosed its way into Village Bay, was stunned by the explosion, though not too stunned to note 'the natives running down Aois-mheall [Oiseval] like a flock of goats, running for their lives – all bare-headed, bare-footed, and coats off'.

The islanders soon regained their composure, for they launched their boat and came alongside, asking if their minister, Neil Mackenzie, was aboard. He had been to the mainland to procure further stores and building materials for the new houses. The first of the *Vulcan*'s boats was launched at 11.30 a.m. and young MacLean was the first to leap ashore on the rocks where landings took place, near the Point of Coll, before the erection of the jetty in 1902.

Among her passengers, the *Vulcan* carried two eminent reverend gentlemen, Dr Norman MacLeod of St Columba's, Glasgow, and Dr David Dickson of St Cuthbert's, Edinburgh, both of whom played leading roles in the formation of the Free Church five years later. The latter was not so nimble in jumping from the boat, and fell into the roaring surf, being soaked to the skin from the waist down. MacLean instantly renamed Village Bay 'Dickson's Bay' and, out of tribute to his colleague, Glen Bay was renamed MacLeod's Bay. These names were ephemeral and never found permanent record on any map, though the letters MacLean wrote to his wife Agnes were headed 'Dickson's Bay, St Kilda'.

Understandably MacLean's letters were almost entirely taken up with descriptions of St Kilda, its stupendous scenery ('like three Ailsa Craigs rolled into one'), its birds and, above all, its 'natives'. Himself a native of Coll and an elder of St Columba's in Govan, he was a fluent Gaelic speaker and devoted a large part of one letter to a sermon by Neil Mackenzie which he took down verbatim. But of the ship itself and its amenities he had very little to say. The overnight accommodation was very spartan – that much we may glean from MacLean's reference to everyone snoring loudly while he was still awake.

The ship weighed anchor early on the Monday and, by 11 p.m., was berthed at Oban. 'Is this a dream or a reality?' he wrote to his wife. 'Have I been in St Kilda this morning, and am I now at 11 o'clock at night in Oban, and reading the *Glasgow Herald* of this morning's date? It is a reality, for I see all my fellow-passengers around me…' All, that is, except Dr MacLeod, who they had dropped off at Fiunary three hours earlier, 'with sky rockets and roar of cannon' of course.

One of the passengers left the ship at Oban to go north to Inverness so MacLean and some others went ashore to give him a 'Scotch convoy'. It must have been near midnight when they headed for the Caledonian Hotel, where they ordered three bottles of whisky and some sugar to make into toddy, consumed by MacConnell and all the male passengers (except Dr Dickson).

MacLean was outraged that the hotel should have charged them 6s a bottle, and resolved never to patronise it again. 'Our excellent and attentive steward, Mr Rose, would have given us as good on board' for half the price. The *Vulcan* got up steam and weighed anchor about 3 a.m., and was back in Glasgow by 8 a.m.

Two

The Navy to
the Rescue

At a time when the Royal Navy was master of the seas, it would not be surprising to learn that the ships of Her Majesty Queen Victoria should occasionally visit St Kilda. In fact, the island had received a visitation in the summer of 1746 when the hunt was on for the fugitive Bonnie Prince Charlie. In mid-June that year a veritable armada of sailing vessels set out to track down the elusive prince, and the rumour that he had taken refuge on St Kilda brought two forty-two-gun warships, the *Loo* and the *Eltham*, along with HMS *Furnace*, *Trial* and *Terror*, as well as a number of troop-carrying wherries. This flotilla anchored in Village Bay on 19 June 1746 and sent ashore parties of marines and soldiers to scour the island.

These were sailing ships, of course, and sail was still predominant up to the middle of the nineteenth century. On 30 June 1840 the ornithologist William MacGillivray reached the island by sailing boat from the Sound of Harris and, in his account, he mentions, in passing, that the 'gun-brig' *Prince of Wales* was anchored in the bay, along with the yacht belonging to the tacksman (tenant), Donald MacDonald of Skeabost, Skye. The 'gun-brig' was a fourteen-gun sloop of 248 tons, built at the Bombay Dockyard in 1805. Very little is known of her later career but the term 'gun-brig' was commonly used in the early nineteenth century for small armed vessels responsible for coastguard and fishery protection duties, and it seems probable that this *Prince of Wales*, the fourth Royal Naval vessel to bear this illustrious name, was engaged in such work when she briefly visited St Kilda in 1840. Indeed, she may well have called there on other occasions, though none has been recorded.

The most important of early visits to St Kilda (mainly because it resulted in the most detailed description of the island up to that time, published the following year) was that paid by Sir Thomas Dick Lauder, Secretary of the Fisheries Board, and the Rev. James Wilson of the Scottish Society for the Propagation of Christian Knowledge. On the afternoon of 17 June 1841 they embarked in the *Princess Royal*, 'a beautiful new cutter of 103 tons, built by Government... for the fishery service'. Although paddle steamers were ten a penny by that time, this handsome vessel was entirely powered by her sails, a point which Wilson noted with some satisfaction: 'We were, indeed, well pleased to exchange the noise and tumult of a Glasgow steamer, with its perpetual throbbing pulse and frequent boisterous breathing, for the tranquil order, comparatively roomy space, and cleanly keeping of the *Princess Royal*.'

It was, in fact, this Government cutter's maiden voyage, and it would take Wilson all round the coasts of Scotland, although the visit to St Kilda, on 2 August, was the high point. Describing this, however, he mentioned the stormy days and contrary winds that had delayed their passage. The days of sail were clearly numbered, although this continued to be the preferred medium for travelling to and from St Kilda by the tacksmen and later the factors of MacLeod of MacLeod, and there are various references in the copious literature of the island to such yachts as the *Rover's Bride,* the *Jessie* (in which Osgood Mackenzie and his mother travelled in 1853), the *Cornwallis*, the sloop *Fowey* (in which Thomas Muir journeyed from Stornoway in 1858) and the factor's smack *Robert Hadden*, which sailed from Dunvegan each year to collect the rents.

In 1844 the Free Church of Scotland, created a year earlier as a result of the Disruption of the General Assembly, launched the *Breadalbane*, a 30 ton schooner designed specifically for carrying missionary work to the remoter parts of the Highlands and Islands. Between 1846 and 1853 she made four trips to St Kilda. Significantly, she was disposed of in the latter year, her relatively high running costs outweighing her usefulness at a time when steamship services were becoming more frequent and far-reaching.

Not that the burgeoning steamers of the West Highlands were making their way to remote St Kilda. An isolated incident took place on Thursday 30 September 1852, when the steamer *Islay* called at Village Bay and embarked eight families, numbering thirty-six men, women and children. She was chartered from the Islay Steam Packet Co. to convey about 400 people from the famine-ridden island of Skye, but among them were a close-knit group, conspicuous by their healthy well-fed appearance. Commenting on the latter's arrival at the Broomielaw, the *Glasgow Herald* wrote: 'This is the first emigration from that remote quarter and we think the cause of humanity would be served if it continued until all the inhabitants have been removed from that barren rock and since so much difficulty exists in disposing of convicted criminals, St Kilda might then be turned with advantage into a penal settlement.' The *Islay*, the first of three steamers to bear that name, was an iron paddle steamer built by Tod & McGregor and launched in 1849. She had a gross tonnage of 325 and was a handsome ship, clipper-bowed and two-masted, with a single funnel abaft the paddle boxes. She was normally employed on the route between West Loch Tarbert, Argyll and the island of Islay but extended operations as far north as Skye and Lewis from 1851 and south to Glasgow. She ran aground in 1866 but was later re-floated and changed her name to *Dolphin* on her acquisition by David Hutcheson & Co.

Sir John MacLeod, the proprietor of St Kilda at that time, came to Glasgow to see his tenants off on the *Princess Royal*, which took them to Birkenhead on 2 October. Thence they sailed off with hundreds of other emigrants bound for Australia but, sadly, half of them died on the voyage, exposed to measles and other diseases from which they had no immunity. This was a devastating blow. It deterred other families from following suit, but the migration nevertheless reduced the remaining population of the island to seventy, and initiated the slow decline that would culminate in the evacuation in August 1930.

In 1859 a sum of money, later known as the Kelsall Fund, was transmitted to the Highland and Agricultural Society of Scotland, a bequest from Charles Kelsall of Hythe (who died in 1857) for the purpose of relieving distress among the inhabitants of the more remote of the Western Isles. Interestingly, he singled out St Kilda for special attention. Kelsall, a bachelor, inherited a fortune from his father who had made his money in India, and seems to have spent his life collecting books and travelling extensively, although there is no record of him actually having been to St Kilda. John Hall Maxwell, the society's secretary, agreed that some of the money could be used advantageously to help the St Kildans, and decided to visit the island to ascertain for himself the most practical uses for the fund. Maxwell initially approached acquaintances who were Commissioners of the Northern Lights. They had their own steamer, the *Pharos*, which regularly served the lighthouses and beacons around the Scottish coast. The only lighthouse in the Outer Hebrides at this time was at Barra Head (1833) and it would not have taken the ship far out of its way to visit St

Kilda, but the commissioners turned Maxwell down flat. Similar applications to the commissioners in subsequent years, right up until 1930, when St Kilda was evacuated, were automatically rejected, although such a stance was increasingly difficult to justify after lighthouses were erected at the Butt of Lewis (1862), the Monach Islands (1864) and the Flannan Isles (1899) – all within a few hours steaming of Hirta. In the early 1870s the *Pharos* did make one visit to St Kilda with the Commissioners of Northern Lights aboard, but this was out of curiosity only and had no philanthropic motives.

Earlier in 1859 the sailing boat used by the factor, Norman MacRaild, was wrecked by an onshore gale at Village Bay, thereby detaining him and a party of workmen who had been sent out to the island by the Free Church to carry out repairs on the church and manse. The failure of these men to return to Skye resulted in the alarm being raised and, apparently for the first time, the help of the Royal Navy being enlisted.

For several years the Navy had been engaged in a hydrographic survey of the Scottish coasts. Chiefly associated with this work were two naval officers who left their mark on St Kilda in the mid-nineteenth century. Lieutenant (later Captain) Frederick W.L. Thomas commanded the *Woodlark*, which surveyed the west coast of Harris and must often have seen St Kilda on the horizon. His wife was a prominent member of the Free Church Ladies' Association and for several years was involved in the supply of books and clothing to the St Kildans. There is no record of the *Woodlark* visiting St Kilda but, in the summer of 1860, Thomas and his wife visited the island aboard HMS *Porcupine*.

This 460 ton wooden gunboat was a paddle steamer-cum-sailing ship which has earned a cherished place in the annals of natural science. In 1869 she made history by carrying out the first deep-water dredge, bringing to the surface organisms from a depth of 5,000m – an event that was almost as earth-shattering as Darwin's theory of evolution, and which prompted the great *Challenger* Expedition of 1872–6, the greatest oceanographic expedition of all time. She was built at Deptford in 1844 specifically for survey duties. She had two funnels, fore and aft of the machinery, two masts and a bowsprit. Apart from the period of the Crimean War (1854–6) when she was stationed in the Baltic, she spent most of her thirty-seven-year career in home waters. In 1859 Captain (later Rear Admiral) Henry C. Otter was appointed her commander and was engaged in the survey of the deeply indented coasts of North Uist when the alarm call was sounded. On reaching Hirta, Otter found the missing factor and the workmen safe and well, albeit running low on food. Their boat had been wrecked within hours of their arrival and they were resigned to spending the long winter months on the desolate isle.

The appearance of the island and its people made a very deep impression on Otter, a man noted for conducting twice-daily religious services aboard ship and his life-long attempts to wean his crews off alcohol in any form. Concerned for the moral and spiritual welfare of the islanders, and more particularly the lack of dependable communications, he submitted a report to the Admiralty recommending that a ship should be sent thither on a regular basis. Their Lordships proved dilatory in considering this request, but Otter was the man on the spot and acted on his own initiative. As a result, HMS *Porcupine* left Portree in Skye at 8 a.m. on Friday 1 June. On board was a rather mixed bunch of passengers – the Rev. James Reid, Free Church minister for Portree, accompanied by two of his elders, and Hall Maxwell of the Highland and Agricultural Society, accompanied by the Duke of Atholl. His Grace was president of the society, and hoped to get some good shooting on the island.

By nightfall on the first day, the ship had managed to cross the Minch in a strong wind, visit Obbe (now Leverburgh) and anchor for the night off Vallay on the north coast of North Uist. A glimpse of their ultimate destination, with Boreray 'floating like a filmy cloud', as Maxwell poetically described it in his journal, seemed to augur well for the following day, but soon after the ship weighed anchor at first light (3 a.m.) and headed out of the Sound of Harris, a north-easterly gale sprang up. Maxwell was a poor sailor and prolonged sea-sickness gave him a jaundiced view of Hirta. The Duke, on the other hand, had an appetite all the more ravening for the buffeting of the wind, and was in excellent spirits when they reached the haven of Village Bay at last.

The Duke, Maxwell and Otter went ashore first, followed some time afterwards by the minister and his elders to hold a service at noon, but no one answered the tolling of the bell, as the women were too busy milking cows and the men would not attend the service without them. Mr Reid had to postpone his prayer meeting until nightfall. When it did get under way, however, it lasted fully four hours.

The clerical party spent the night ashore, accommodated by Duncan Kennedy, the catechist, in the manse. The following day, being the Sabbath, was given over entirely to church services ('all in Gaelic', as Maxwell, who understood not a word of that language, sourly observed). As usual, the Duke was in excellent spirits and, discovering that Reid was a native of Ballechin, was pleased to find a fellow Perthshire man.

On the first night the Duke slept in his cabin aboard ship, but on Sunday night he and Macdonald of Balranald (North Uist) elected to spend the night 'on the floor of one of the cottages, which is still pointed out as the place of his shelter'. It should be remembered that the village in 1860 consisted solely of the thatched cottages erected in the late 1830s and it was not until the following year that work on the sixteen houses facing the sea commenced. Doubtless it gave Maxwell some satisfaction to observe that His Grace and his interpreter were obliged to lie down 'in an atmosphere as offensive as peat smoke, and the odour of oil, feathers, and birds could make it'. His *schadenfreude* was dented by the Duke's obvious enjoyment of the experience: 'His Grace, whom no roughing nor discomfort can disconcert, was delighted at having achieved his object.'

Maxwell noted smugly that Macdonald was not as happy as the Duke but felt obliged to go along with this daft notion, otherwise His Grace would not have been able to communicate with his hosts. As they were accommodated in the cottage of Malcolm Macdonald and his wife Betty Scott (an English-speaking 'incomer'), the Duke would have managed perfectly well. Indeed, he noted in his diary that 'Betty, our Landlady, was the only one on shore who could speak English'. Betty, popularly known as the Queen of St Kilda, was a native of Lochinver in Wester Ross, and her Lowland surname suggests that she was the daughter of one of the Borders shepherds who had migrated northwards in the 1790s. She had come to St Kilda with the Rev. Neil Mackenzie in the early 1830s, probably as housekeeper to his wife and young family.

The Duke would quite happily have spent a second night ashore, but Captain Otter, apprehensive of the weather, which was worsening again, eventually persuaded him to go aboard. At 5 a.m. the following morning the *Porcupine* got under way and reached Rodel in South Harris by mid-afternoon. While the Duke went off to shoot seals, Maxwell and Reid made a pilgrimage to the ruined (but now restored) church of St Clement. The ship returned to her home port of Portree on Wednesday and the Duke and Maxwell hosted a dinner for Otter and his officers at the hotel.

Two weeks later, the *Porcupine* was back in Village Bay. On this occasion Lieutenant and Mrs Thomas were guests of Captain Otter and with them was Thomas's assistant, the surveyor Henry Sharbau, whose own niche in the island's story was secured by his detailed map of the houses and crofts – an invaluable record of the village immediately prior to the erection of the 'modern' houses. Between these two visits Otter had written to the Admiralty strongly advising the creation of a proper landing place. He explained that the islanders were compelled to haul boats up on a sloping shelf at the north-eastern side of the bay, an extremely hazardous operation even in ideal weather conditions and quite impossible at other times. He suggested that an inlet, at present choked with large boulders, be cleared out and a crane be erected at the top of the nearby cliff, so that boats could be lifted out of the water. This eminently practical solution was not carried out until fully forty years had passed, although in the long run it was improved by the addition of the jetty.

He stated that Maxwell was prepared to recommend to his committee the expenditure of £100 on this project. The jetty, completed in 1902, cost rather more than £600. Otter concluded his very long and detailed report with the information that Hall Maxwell was proposing 'to build new houses more commodious in size, which proposition gives great satisfaction and they all agreed to put up the walls themselves'.

During the *Porcupine*'s second visit to St Kilda in the summer of 1860 Captain Thomas, armed with a whole-plate camera, took the opportunity to photograph the island and its inhabitants – providing the earliest known images. Thomas was indefatigable in his quest for all manner of information about St Kilda and it was due to his efforts that much of the oral tradition of the island was recorded. Between them, Otter and Thomas played a major role in the advancement of the material wellbeing of St Kilda, in the best traditions of the Royal Navy, going far beyond the call of mere duty.

On 27 September 1860 the *Porcupine*, then engaged in taking soundings of the ocean westward of North Uist, returned to the island and anchored for the night in Village Bay. Lieutenant Hawes, the ship's 'number one' checked up on the progress being made by the workmen sent thither by the Highland Society to carry out the work recommended by Hall Maxwell. On this occasion the ship remained for several days, her crew assisting the workmen in moving the heavy boulders to create a breakwater. On the evening of 2 October, as the barometer fell and the wind strengthened from the south-east, the ship got up steam and headed round to Glen Bay for shelter. About 2 a.m. the following morning Otter decided to return to Village Bay. As the ship rounded the north coast a hurricane arose suddenly from the north-west and the *Porcupine* was caught on a lee shore. Hawes subsequently reported:

In vain was the helm put hard-a-port, and the engines turned on full-speed, the ship was on her beam ends, and both engines and helm were powerless. Finding which, the dangerous experiment of turning astern full speed was tried – dangerous because the rudder might go at any moment, or the ship become pooped – but even this seemed to have little effect. The sea was one mass of foam and spray, with a lurid glare all round. The weather paddle-box boat was blown off the box in-board, but fortunately was brought up by the upright davits which are used for hoisting her out. Had this not been the case the foremost funnel must have gone, and the ship would then have been on fire. All the binnacle lights were either blown out or dashed to pieces, tiller ropes carried away, boats' oars, rudders, and other small things flying about with dangerous velocity in all directions. For two hours the storm raged with unparalleled fury, and although so close as the ship must have been to the island nothing could be seen of it.

Fortunately the *Porcupine* narrowly averted total shipwreck and rode out the storm. However, when the wind abated and the ship was able to re-enter Village Bay, the crew found a scene of utter devastation. Most of the houses had been unroofed, the corn stooks had been blown into the sea and the islanders' boat was smashed to smithereens. It was providential that the *Porcupine* was there at the time, as the islanders could be provisioned with dried meat and ship's biscuit while tarpaulins and spare sails were hastily improvised as shelters until the roofs could be repaired. This was one of the worst storms ever recorded in the Highlands and it caused immense damage from eastern Perthshire to south-western Argyll.

The account by Hawes was published in the *Inverness Courier*. Otter wrote in similar vein to Maxwell who passed his letter to the *Glasgow Herald* with an appeal for money to aid the stricken island. The Kelsall Fund was not inexhaustible and, besides, it took some time to release money from it. In the meantime, so much cash flowed in from all over the British Isles as a result of the newspaper appeal that the cargo steamer *Islesman*, chartered for a special sailing to St Kilda on 29 October, could not take all the stores which had been accumulated, and concentrated mainly on foodstuffs and materials for roof repairs.

Maxwell had come to the conclusion that the St Kildans would benefit considerably from a new boat, the loss of the existing boat as a result of the hurricane making this imperative. This was a fishing vessel with a length of 30ft, equipped with a mast and lugsail, constructed by Darroch & Espie of Glasgow at a total cost of £50 16s 6d, including freight to St Kilda. In due course, this was supplied, and named the *Dargavel* after Maxwell's mansion near Bishopton, Renfrewshire. On her maiden voyage to North Uist she almost foundered, due to clumsy handling by her inexperienced crew. In April 1863 she set sail for Harris with a crew of seven men and Betty Scott as interpreter. The boat was lost with all hands, in the most suspicious circumstances. Suspicion fell on some English sailors, and foul play was suspected when some clothing was allegedly discovered in a sea-girt cave at Mealasta in north-west Lewis some time afterwards. But boxes containing cloth and birds' feathers were also washed ashore and suggested shipwreck, although no bodies were ever found. Fourteen years later news of one of the missing men came from Lydenburg in the Transvaal. Apparently he had just died and left a sum of money to be remitted to his elderly father. It later transpired that the dead man was a native of Lewis and had no connection with St Kilda, and to this day the mystery of the *Dargavel* remains unsolved.

In June 1861 the *Porcupine* was back at St Kilda, this time on official business, having onboard Alexander Grigor from Inverness, the Examiner of Registers for the Northern District of Scotland. Although the national census had been taken every ten years since 1841, this was the first time that Britain's remotest island was properly recorded. Captain Otter probably made other journeys out to St Kilda in the ensuing years. In September 1864 he was on hand to convey a theological student, Alexander Cameron, to the island as catechist, not only carrying him from Lochboisdale aboard the *Porcupine* but also making sure that the manse was rendered comfortable for him. Otter, who was deeply attached to the islanders, also took the opportunity to visit each family in turn and minister to the sick.

Otter also visited St Kilda aboard the gunboat *Seagull* in June 1863 (presumably the *Porcupine* was undergoing repairs or a refit at the time). On this occasion he was accompanied by Mrs Thomas, who spent twenty hours ashore. This was only about two months after the *Dargavel* disappeared, and Otter was shocked to find the islanders in a state of great despondency.

The example set by Otter and Thomas was followed by other naval officers in the ensuing decades. In February 1866 HMS *Jackal*, commanded by Captain Dyer, made her first voyage to St Kilda, bringing out the Rev. John Mackay, the first ordained minister to serve on the island since the departure of Neil Mackenzie after the Disruption. A native of Jeantown in Wester Ross and formerly a schoolmaster, he was fifty when he entered his encumbency, having apparently been ordained for this specific task. He would impose a gloomy, at times harsh, regime on his tiny flock and his extreme, dour form of Calvinism has often been blamed for the decline of St Kilda. The paddle steamer HMS *Harpy* (Captain Bell) was at St Kilda in 1869, followed by the fishery cruiser HMS *Vigilant* (Captain Macdonald) which paid several visits in the early 1870s.

The *Jackal*, based at Stornoway and now under the command of Lieutenant Commander W. Digby, paid several visits to St Kilda in that decade, most notably in February 1877 when it rescued the crew of the Austrian barquentine *Peti Dubrovacki* which had been wrecked at Rockall. The Christian charity and Highland hospitality shown by the St Kildans, poor people on the very margins of subsistence, in taking in the shipwrecked strangers – and Papists at that – as well as clothing, sheltering and feeding them over the winter, when they had so very little food for themselves, stirred the hearts of the nation when the story broke in the newspapers. Appeals for help for the islanders produced an immediate and generous response, following the example of the Austrian government which, in mid-April, sent £100 to the Highland and Agricultural Society to procure supplies for St Kilda.

Fletcher Menzies, who had just succeeded Hall Maxwell as secretary of the society, obtained the services of the Royal Navy, this time in the shape of HMS *Flirt*, a gunboat in the squadron headed by the battleship *Arethusa*, then based in the Firth of Clyde. Under the command of Lieutenant O'Rorke, the ship left Greenock on Thursday 10 May and reached St Kilda late on the Saturday evening. On board was John MacDiarmid, a junior official of the Highland Society, who compiled a detailed account of the voyage and description of the island and its inhabitants, which was subsequently published. One thing that struck both O'Rorke and MacDiarmid forcibly was the stout refusal of the minister and his elders to allow the ship to be unloaded that night, so close to the Sabbath.

Naval planning had not taken any account of the extreme Sabbatarianism of the St Kildans, otherwise the voyage might have been rescheduled to mid-week. Mindful of the capricious weather conditions (which had already given the *Flirt* a hard time rounding the Mull of Kintyre) O'Rorke was adamant that the stores must be unloaded immediately or not at all; he was not prepared to hang about until Monday morning, but must put out to sea if conditions worsened again. The islanders countered: so be it – they were quite prepared to hazard a trip in open boats to Harris to pick up the stores there if the Navy dropped them off at Obbe. O'Rorke tried to break this impasse by landing stores with the ship's boats but, without any assistance from the islanders, this proved an impossible feat. In the end he conceded defeat and returned to his ship to wait for Monday. Barely an hour after midnight on Sunday, however, the St Kildans set to with great vigour and by dawn all the stores had been safely brought ashore, enabling the gunboat to depart at 7.30 a.m.

Diplomatically, MacDiarmid went ashore and sought the hospitality of the manse on Saturday night and, accompanied by some of the ship's officers and crew, dutifully attended all three religious services the following day. The enforced delay also afforded MacDiarmid a greater opportunity to inspect the island in general and the houses in particular, compiling his own census of the inhabitants and providing more detail than the official decennial census. Meanwhile, Staff Surgeon Scott examined the islanders, noting their general condition as well as treating the sick and injured; his medical assessment formed an invaluable appendix to MacDiarmid's report. When it was published in due course it proved a useful antidote to the vituperations of John Sands, whose book *Out of the World, or Life on St Kilda* had created a stir in 1876 and even more heated controversy when the revised edition appeared in 1878. It was a tendentious work which unfairly lambasted the proprietor and the minister alike (the latter was cruelly caricatured in one of the Sands drawings), but it had the positive effect of focusing public attention on St Kilda. Up to 1876, few people had heard of the island, but after that date it would seldom be out of the news. It was undoubtedly a watershed in the island's history, for good or ill.

The resulting publicity induced Miss Emily MacLeod of MacLeod to petition the Admiralty about sending this ship to St Kilda on a regular basis. However, this was rejected on the grounds that St Kilda was the property of a private individual (her brother) and within the jurisdiction of the Parochial Board of Harris, and therefore 'it is not considered that the services of HM ships should be called into requisition to supply the needs of a civil population'. Nevertheless, on other occasions the Navy would come to the rescue of St Kilda when the islanders were confronted by famine or struck down by disease, and in the end it was HMS *Harebell* which would evacuate them to the mainland in August 1930.

If the Admiralty of the 1870s was no longer inclined to turn a blind eye to the benevolent free enterprise of its captains in regard to St Kilda, help was just around the corner. The era of the commercial steamer was about to begin.

Three

The Advent of the
Dunara Castle

A part from naval vessels and the annual visitation of the factor in his smack, the *Robert Hadden*, St Kilda was increasingly the destination of private yachts. In the summer of 1873 William Young brought his wife and family to St Kilda aboard his steam yacht *Nyanza*. It seems possible that Young was the son of a ship-owner of the same name who had been engaged in the West Highland trade in the 1830s before forming a short-lived partnership with George Burns in 1835, resulting in Burns acquiring both of Young's steamers, *Inverness* and *Rob Roy*, in September the same year. On this occasion, the Young family were accompanied by some friends, including Dr R. Angus Smith who subsequently published a narrative of the voyage, first serialised in the periodical *Good Words* (1875) and later released in a revised edition as a single volume (1879), complete with a real photograph of the yacht in Village Bay by way of a frontispiece. On that occasion the minister went through his usual routine of appealing to the strangers for help for 'the poor people of this island'. Smith considered that he had not seen such 'bright-eyed, fat and comfortable, and well-fed' people anywhere in the Highlands, so John Mackay's appeal fell on deaf ears. To be sure, the usual gifts of sweets and tobacco were doled out, as well as some fishing lines. Furthermore, Young gave way to the minister's importuning and promised the islanders a new boat. This was duly delivered the following summer, being towed out to St Kilda by the factor's new smack, the *Janet*, aboard which John Sands of Ormiston, a radical journalist and all-round troublemaker, was a passenger.

In August 1874 the steam yacht *Griffin* set out from Loch Nevis near Mallaig with passengers and crew numbering sixteen souls, including Sir William Baillie of Polkemmet and his wife, the celebrated authoress, who duly sent the obligatory account to *The Home and Foreign Missionary Record* of the Church of Scotland. Significantly, she commented on the fact that, far from rushing enthusiastically to greet the new arrivals, the islanders were at first nowhere to be seen, only after some time emerging from their cottages, having taken the trouble to don their Sunday best before coming down to the shore. Lady Baillie's desire to play 'lady bountiful' was somewhat dashed by the arrival of a second steam yacht, the *Calder*, soon afterwards. Two steamers in a single day! What next? The *Calder* was exceptional, if not unique, in not generating the usual rather patronising screed that the newspapers and magazines of the period seem to have been so eager to publish.

In July 1875 the yacht *Crusader*, owned and skippered by Sir Patrick Keith-Murray, anchored in Village Bay. While Sir Patrick headed for the cliffs and a demonstration of spectacular cragsmanship, John Sands cadged a lift back to the mainland. Unlike most of the yachts now frequenting the island, *Crusader* was totally reliant on wind power and thus the return journey to Gourock, via Barra Head, Skerryvore and Rathlin Island, was very slow on account of the relatively calm weather. The visit of the *Crusader* may have been quite accidental as the customary presents were not distributed to the expectant St Kildans, but subsequently Sir Patrick despatched a couple of wooden chandeliers for the church and two clocks, apparently the first timepieces ever on the island.

Early in August that year, a yacht visited St Kilda which seems to have been a portent of things to come, for the brief note which appeared in *The Scotsman* of 13 August described it as 'a business cruise', which indicates that the sixteen passengers had paid for the privilege rather than being aboard as guests of the owner. Perhaps the weather had not been too clement, for this anonymous account is the most jaundiced ever published, its main thrust being that a subscription 'should be got up for the removal of these seventy-two persons from their lazy, stupid and dirty life in the island' and their place taken by goats and sheep. One of the passengers was an eminent physician, Dr Murchison of Harris, who spent his entire time ashore giving urgent medical treatment to the islanders. As a result, he paid a second visit before the year was out to see how his patients were faring.

During the winter of 1876–7 John Sands waged a vendetta against the MacLeod of MacLeod, accusing him of 'landlordism', shameless exploitation and gross neglect of his tenants on lone St Kilda. Norman MacLeod of MacLeod, who had only recently purchased the island from Sir John MacPherson MacLeod and brought it back within the ancestral dominions of the clan chief out of sentiment, lived and worked in London where he had risen to eminence in the South Kensington Museum. He had to admit that he had never visited the island and thus Sands invariably wrong-footed him in the verbal duel conducted in the pages of various newspapers and periodicals.

Back at Dunvegan, however, resided Norman's sister, Miss Emily MacLeod of MacLeod. She supported him to the hilt, but realised that the only way to give the lie to Sands and his allegations was to visit St Kilda and spend some time there. Accordingly, in the spring of 1877, she originally planned to journey thither aboard the factor's smack. In the end, however, she decided that it would be more politic to make her way there independently of the factor, John Mackenzie, and accepted an invitation from Lord and Lady Macdonald in their steam yacht *Lord of the Isles* which left Sleat at the southern tip of Skye on Thursday 15 June and picked her up at Dunvegan at 4 p.m. The voyage across the Minch was very calm and enjoyable, but once they had passed through the Sound of Harris they encountered the long Atlantic swell which, even in calm weather, was a sore trial to poor sailors, and as a result both Emily and Lady Macdonald were very sick. Mercifully they anchored in Village Bay at 2 a.m. the following morning. 'Was not that quick?' she posed rhetorically in a letter to her sister Mary. On this voyage they were accompanied by the Rev. Archibald MacNeill, minister of Sleat, and Donald Macdonald of Tormore who knew St Kilda well, having been the factor for the previous owner, Sir John MacPherson MacLeod.

The party went ashore at 10 a.m. and Miss Emily moved into the factor's house where she spent a fortnight on the island. She had originally intended to spend a month there, but her plans were curtailed by delays in the Macdonalds making their own preparations. Nevertheless, the two weeks she spent there proved of immense value, both in the short term and for the future. Apart from the ongoing feud between her brother and the egregious Sands, which impelled Emily to redress any genuine grievances felt by the islanders, her long-term goal was an improvement in the health and welfare of the St Kildans. In particular, she was appalled at the high infant mortality rate and over the ensuing years would labour long and hard to provide St Kilda with a trained nurse.

Their arrival coincided with the annual visit of John Mackenzie, who had sailed in the *Robert Hadden* direct from Dunvegan. While Emily occupied the two downstairs rooms the factor had the upper floor (approached by a separate door at the back of the house) while he conducted his business with the islanders. Soon, both the steam yacht and the factor's smack departed and Emily was left, like Lady Grange, on her own, although in infinitely better conditions than that poor demented woman who had been kidnapped by her ex-husband's cronies and marooned on St Kilda from 1734 to 1741. Soon after her arrival Emily inspected the stone hut where Lady Grange had been incarcerated and this sent a chill through her body. A fear of being stranded on St Kilda was a recurring theme of her letters home. In her first letter to her sister Mary, Emily speculated about how she would get off the island: 'It would be dangerous to wait for a yacht, as many of them didn't go to Skye at all but down by Barra Head to Glasgow.'

In fact, another yacht arrived at St Kilda on 16 June. It was owned by a man named Clare, and Emily gave her sister an interesting account of her conversations with the islanders as they speculated what he was worth and how much he might give them, comparing the largesse given by Mr Young with that distributed by Lord and Lady Macdonald. When Clare only handed over £1 they dismissed him as 'a very hard man', though it was twice the sum given by Lord Macdonald. As the cash was evenly divided among all seventeen families, Emily concluded that Lord Macdonald had given them sevenpence each, while Mr Clare gave 1s 2d. Twenty years of visiting yachts carrying wealthy owners had already had a corrupting influence.

But much worse was to come. Emily concluded her letter of 16 June, 'I mean to come back by *Dunara* on the 2nd July'. The impending arrival of the steamer with a large party of excursionists was regarded with mixed feelings. While many of the islanders were excited at the prospect of trading hand-knitted stockings and homespuns to the *daoine-uasal*, the more thoughtful were apprehensive, and this view was reinforced by the minister who, on Sunday 1 July, preached a powerful sermon 'on the dangers of bad companionship'. Emily confided to her sister that 'as no one on the island could be called a bad companion everyone recognised that Mr Sands must have been on his brain'. Sands had apparently promised to come back to St Kilda and claim the hand of young Marion Gillies with whom he had fallen in love during his enforced exile on the island.

Emily herself was apprehensive about the ship's arrival as the last thing she wanted was an unpleasant confrontation with her brother's arch enemy. Fortunately, Sands was conspicuously absent from the throng of passengers that came ashore the following day. In fact, he never returned to St Kilda and Marion's parents were relieved, though angry that Sands had taken away a large consignment of knitted goods which he promised to sell on the mainland on their behalf.

Very little appears to be known of the Orme family which became a household name in the West Highlands and Islands as a result of their shipping operations. The name is of Scandinavian origin, meaning a serpent (hence the English word 'worm'). Apart from numerous instances in Scandinavia its name may be found as far afield as Germany (Ormesheim) and France (Ormesson), but most placenames derived from it are in those parts of Scotland and England which were occupied by the Vikings, such as Ormidale, Ormsary and Ormsaig in the West Highlands and numerous locations with the prefix Arm-, Orm- or Urm- in England. The progenitors of the steamship company were James, Martin and Laurence, who began trading as Orme Bros in January 1853 with the iron-hulled three-masted screw steamer *Queen*, built a few months earlier by Thomas Wingate of Glasgow. She had a gross tonnage of 275 and was originally intended for the route all the way from Glasgow to Stornoway, but only ran as far as Portree in Skye. After six months' operation the ship was withdrawn from service and sold to a company trading on the coast of Victoria, Australia.

Nothing further is known of the original company, but the middle brother, Martin, was appointed general manager of the Great West of Scotland Fishery Co. in April 1857 and thus superintended the operations of the steamship *Islesman*, built by Robert Napier in 1858 as a fish transporter, serving the company's various fishing stations. As we shall see later, fish are capricious creatures that tend to change their habitat suddenly and for no apparent reason. This phenomenon gravely affected the company's operations in the Minch and the North Sea and it went into liquidation in 1860. The *Islesman* was disposed of to a Glasgow businessman, William Lang, who entered into a partnership with Martin Orme. In 1861 the ship, substantially lengthened and otherwise modernised, began operating as a passenger and cargo vessel between Glasgow and the Western Isles, calling at many ports which had never seen a steamer before. Martin Orme is credited with this enterprising venture. Orme had other interests at this period, being the joint-owner of the screw steamship *Scotia* with Alexander A. Laird, whose father and uncle, the brothers Alexander and John Laird, had been partners with Archibald MacConnell in the 1820s.

The *Islesman* was sold in 1866 and replaced two years later by the 230 ton coastal vessel, appropriately named *Dunvegan Castle* after the stronghold of the MacLeods. By the 1870s this ship was neither large enough nor sufficiently seaworthy for the robust conditions of the West Coast trade. In 1875 she ran aground at Dunvegan and, although she was successfully re-floated, she was sold off soon afterwards. Thereafter, for many years, she was operated by J. Mawson of Barrow-in-Furness, until April 1889, when she sank, following a collision in

Mersey estuary. At the time of her mishap on the rocks overlooked by the ancient castle whose name she bore, Martin Orme was already ordering a larger and more powerful replacement. This was the *Dunara Castle*, named after a medieval ruin on the west coast of Mull. She was built by Blackwood & Gordon of Port Glasgow and was launched in the spring of 1875, shortly after the *Dunvegan Castle* was taken out of service.

She was a vessel of 450 tons and originally had two funnels painted bright red with black tops, and a two-cylinder simple engine. In 1882 she was re-boilered with compound machinery and thereafter appeared with a single funnel. What is misleading is that, from the outset, Orme's steamer handbills showed the image of a ship with a single funnel, but this may have merely been a stock woodcut used by the printer and not intended to convey an accurate impression of the ship herself.

She made her maiden voyage on 21 June 1875, leaving the Broomielaw at 10 a.m. and reaching Greenock by 6 p.m. From there she sailed down the Firth of Clyde, round the Mull of Kintyre, and called at Colonsay, Iona, Bunessan, Tiree and Coll, then crossing the Minch and visiting Castlebay (Barra), Lochboisdale and Carnan (South Uist), Lochmaddy (North Uist) and Rodel and Tarbert (Harris). From there she re-crossed the Minch, calling at Uig, Stein and Dunvegan in Skye. The voyage to Tarbert took about four days and the return about a day less, with a quick turnaround at Glasgow in order to repeat the route exactly a week later. On alternate weeks she also called at a number of other little ports, such as Struan and Carbost in Skye, Obbe in the Sound of Harris, Kallin in the Uists, 'and any other places of Call or Recall that may be agreed upon'.

After two years on this run the *Dunara Castle* had acquired a reputation for punctuality and safety. She was widely admired as 'a handsome ship and a fine sea boat'. Although primarily intended as a cargo vessel, from the outset she offered substantial accommodation for passengers. Originally this provided berths for about forty people, but this was later increased to fifty and latterly more than sixty, by an ingenious system of converting the saloon and other public areas into dormitories, with upper and lower bunks, sofas and even tables being transformed into beds by the end of the day. A modicum of privacy was provided by curtains reminiscent of those in the sleeping cars on trains of the period.

The excursion to St Kilda scheduled for Monday 2 July 1877 was extensively advertised well in advance. According to George Seton, an Edinburgh advocate who had lectured about St Kilda for many years and set the seal on this by making his one and only visit to the island aboard the steamer, there were about forty passengers, including three ladies. Having spent four hours ashore

SS *Dunara Castle* in Village Bay, 1881. Originally fitted with twin funnels, this was reduced to one after she was re-boilered in 1882. Note the galvanised iron roofs of the 1860 houses glinting in the sunlight.

on that historic day he returned to Edinburgh to put the finishing touches to his magnum opus *St Kilda, Past and Present*, which was published by Blackwood the following year. Although decried by rival authors, both then and later, as a scissors-and-paste job, Seton deserves credit for amassing so much material in one place. Inevitably one of his harshest critics was the pugnacious Sands, annoyed at some of Seton's scarcely veiled remarks about him.

A footnote on page 64 of Seton's book enumerates the more important fellow-travellers: 'Captain Macdonald of Waternish; Major James Colquhoun, Arroquhar and a younger brother; Dr George Keith and son, Edinburgh; Mr Bulkeley, Procurator-Fiscal, Lochmaddy; Dr Messer, Helensburgh; Rev. John Macrae, minister of North Uist; Dr Mackenzie, Old Calabar; and Mr Thomas Ormerod, Brighouse.' Also on board was Captain Macdonald of HMS *Vigilant*, having something of a busman's holiday but acting as a guide to his fellow passengers when they reached St Kilda. Seton paid tribute to Captain McEwan and the ship's clerk (purser) Mr Donald 'who did everything in their power to insure an enjoyable expedition'.

They landed at 10 a.m., re-boarded the ship at 2 p.m., and then circumnavigated the group. Seton recalls: 'Although the sea was somewhat heavy outside, we had no difficulty in landing; and the weather was most propitious throughout.'

Seton also mentioned that Miss MacLeod of MacLeod 'accompanied us on our return'. Passengers on the *Dunara Castle* who did not wish to risk the rigours of the trip to St Kilda were obliged to leave the ship at Obbe, and re-boarded when she returned to the Sound of Harris on the homeward voyage.

Although not singled out for the list of the great and good, Seton also mentioned 'Mr W.M. Wilson, who formed one of the party' and who penned 'a graphic account of the entire cruise of the *Dunara* from Glasgow and back' which appeared in nine instalments in the *Ayr Observer* between 24 July and 2 October that year. Long-winded, patronising and full of feeble attempts at humour, this series did not reach St Kilda until halfway through the fifth article. Before they went ashore the tourists were given a pep talk by Captain Macdonald, especially about not being too generous with their cash: 'Don't be profuse… I'm afraid the mistaken kindness of yachting people will demoralise the Islanders. If you scatter your money carelessly, those who come next will pay for your extravagance.' It was decided to pool resources and give £2 to the minister who would divide the money fairly. On leaving the Sound of Harris, the passengers had chipped in half a crown apiece for a 'pot' to be paid to the St Kildans for a display of cliff-climbing.

Wilson's main conclusion was to rubbish the suggestion by John Sands that St Kilda deserved a regular communication with the outside world, in the form of a quarterly visit by a government ship carrying the mails and stores. 'Surely all this is philanthropy and sentiment run mad!' he declaimed, without actually supporting this conclusion with a well-reasoned argument. Like everyone else who visited St Kilda in that period and made instant pronouncements, Wilson adopted a wholly subjective stance which told his readers more about himself than the St Kildans.

The handbill produced by Martin Orme on 17 May 1878 for the June sailings of the *Dunara Castle* contained an announcement in bold lettering:

TOUR TO ST KILDA

To afford Tourists another opportunity of visiting this far-famed island, the Steamer will call there, leaving Glasgow on Thursday, 13th June.

Again, about forty passengers left Dunvegan at 9 a.m. on the Saturday, proceeded at a leisurely pace to Tarbert and then set out early on Monday. An account of this excursion appeared anonymously in three consecutive issues of *The Highlander* (15 to 29 June 1878).

JUNE SAILINGS.

GLASGOW AND THE HIGHLANDS.

The undernoted or other Steamer, is intended to sail with Goods and Passengers, unless prevented by weather or unforeseen circumstances, as under:—

"DUNARA CASTLE,"

From GLASGOW every THURSDAY at 10 A.M.

Train to Greenock (Bridge Street) at 6 p.m.

6th June, TO	13th June, TO	20th June, TO	27th June, TO
COLONSAY	COLONSAY	COLONSAY	COLONSAY
IONA	IONA	IONA	IONA
BUNESSAN	BUNESSAN	BUNESSAN	BUNESSAN
TYREE	TYREE	TYREE	TYREE
COLL	COLL	COLL	COLL
BARRA	STRUAN	BARRA	STRUAN
LOCHBOISDALE	CARBOST	LOCHBOISDALE	CARBOST
CARNAN	DUNVEGAN	CARNAN	DUNVEGAN
LOCHMADDY	UIG	LOCHMADDY	UIG
RODEL	TARBERT	RODEL	TARBERT
TARBERT	OBBE	TARBERT	OBBE
UIG	LOCHMADDY	UIG	LOCHMADDY
STEIN	KALLIN	STEIN	KALLIN
DUNVEGAN	CARNAN	DUNVEGAN	CARNAN
	LOCHBOISDALE		LOCHBOISDALE
	BARRA		BARRA

And any other Places of Call or Recall that may be agreed upon.

Returning to GLASGOW from

TARBERT,	Mondays, 10th & 24th June & 1st July, about 4 A.M.	COLL, every Tuesday, . . .	about 5 A.M.
LOCHBOISDALE,	Fridays, 7th & 21st June, .	,, 11 P.M.	TYREE, ,, . . . |,, 7 ,,
"	Monday, 1st July, . . .	,, 6 P.M.	BUNESSAN, ,, . . .	,, 2 P.M.
DUNVEGAN,	Saturdays, 15th & 29th June, .	,, 5 A.M.	IONA, ,, . . .	,, 2.30 P.M.
"	Mondays, 10th & 24th June, .	,, 6 P.M.	COLONSAY, ,, . . .	,, 6 ,,

TOUR TO ST. KILDA.

To afford Tourists another opportunity of visiting this far-famed island, the Steamer will call there, leaving Glasgow on Thursday, 13th June.

☞ All Freights must be Prepaid.

Senders of Goods from the Country will please give instructions to the Railway Company, or other Carrier, to pay Freight, otherwise the Goods cannot be taken.

NOTE.—As the Steamer is to make a Special Call at the island of St. Kilda on the voyage of 13th June, any Passengers for the South who may have joined previously, and have not booked specially for St. Kilda, will, when the Steamer arrives at Obbe, require to land there, but can join again on the Steamer's return from St. Kilda.

THE undernoted are the only Agents authorised to receive Goods for Shipment. Goods for Shipment at the other Stations will be received by the Clerk on Board the Steamer, who is alone authorised to receive Goods at those places, and grant Receipts for the same.
The Owners reserve the right to vary or alter the Voyages when found necessary, and are not accountable for Passengers' Luggage, nor for empty packages, unless Booked and Freight Prepaid on same, nor for Damage Goods may sustain in Landing or Shipping at Ferries, nor for Goods until actually received on Board, nor for loss or injury to live Stock. The delivery of Goods is complete when they are discharged from the Steamer, after which they are entirely at the risk of the Owners.—Goods may be landed either going North or coming South, as circumstances permit. The Steamer may tow or assist vessels in distress.

For further particulars apply to DONALD M'CORMICK, Custom-House Quay, Greenock, or to

17th May, 1878.   MARTIN ORME, 20 Robertson Street, Glasgow.

All Live Stock must be accompanied by the Owner or his Servant.

The handbill published by Martin Orme for the June 1878 sailings of the *Dunara Castle* with the cruise to St Kilda on 13 June highlighted. Incidentally, the illustration was merely a stock woodcut and did not resemble the ship at that time, as she had two funnels originally.

The last act of John Sands on behalf of the St Kildans, before he lost interest and moved on to pastures new, was to petition the Admiralty to give him one of the longboats, now surplus to naval requirements, which were being offered for sale at Plymouth Dockyard. The Admiralty, having been less than helpful of late, acceded to this request and in due course a jollyboat, complete with sailing equipment and compass, was transported by the *Dunara Castle* to the island, free of charge. When the ship anchored in Village Bay the boat was lowered, and joined one of the existing island boats in ferrying the passengers ashore.

The four hours on the island followed the now strictly prescribed routine: a formal greeting by the minister and Isabella Munro (Mrs Neil Macdonald), the only English speakers; the distribution of sweets and tobacco; a scramble to the summit of Conachair to witness the display of cragsmanship and another scramble down the steep slopes to the village to purchase hand-knitted stockings and gloves; bolts of cloth and specimens of birds' eggs, particularly the much sought after St Kilda wren; and then a nosey round the street, peering into the cottages at the natives in their quaint habitat. There was unanimity that the £1 12s 6d spent on the excursion was worth every penny.

One of the proposals strongly advocated by John Sands was a regular mail service to and from St Kilda. This was something of a side-swipe at John T. Mackenzie, the factor for MacLeod of MacLeod who was also postmaster of Dunvegan. This was a much more important job than it is nowadays for, back in the nineteenth century, Dunvegan ranked as a 'post town' controlling a number of 'receiving houses' (the equivalent of sub post offices in a later generation) in the north and west of Skye. In his role of factor, Mackenzie was committed to making an annual visit to the island, mainly to take out much-needed supplies and collect the island's produce, which also constituted the rent. The cost of despatching his 80 ton schooner *Robert Hadden* was £15, and far outweighed the profit from any trade with the islanders. At no time did Mackenzie receive any payment or subsidy from the General Post Office for conveying the mails to or from St Kilda, although this was one of the proposals put forward by Sands in 1877 and even tentatively considered by the Post Office the following year.

Sands was the prime mover in a meeting held at Edinburgh on 5 March 1877 which resolved that the Government be petitioned to construct a proper landing place at St Kilda and establish regular postal communications. Some weight to these arguments was lent by the fact that, later the same year, the Post Office conceded a fortnightly postal communication between Fair Isle and the mainland of Shetland. Though Fair Isle had just lost half its population through migration, it was much closer to civilisation than St Kilda and the steamers that plied regularly between Orkney and Shetland need make only a slight detour to serve the island.

St Kilda, however, was regarded as far too remote, and the Postmaster General passed the buck to the Lords of the Admiralty who passed the matter in turn to the Home Office and there it apparently reached a dead end. In due course it was referred back to the Post Office for further investigation and thus the problem landed on the desk of Mr Warren, the Surveyor for the Scottish District. An enquiry addressed to John Mackenzie elicited the information that letters addressed to St Kilda frequently lay at Obbe or Dunvegan for months before they were transmitted on the annual visit to collect the rent. On Mackenzie's recommendation, Warren urged that a regular service be instituted by a steamer in the spring and autumn and this, with the factor's visit in mid-summer, would give St Kilda a thrice-yearly service.

This recommendation was passed on to London in due course and, as a result, one of the passengers on the *Dunara* during her cruise of June 1878 was Mr Benthall, an assistant secretary at the General Post Office in London. On this occasion only three letters were delivered and ten collected as the factor had visited St Kilda only a week previously. The writer or recipient of these thirteen letters was John Mackay himself. On this basis, Benthall reckoned that the inward and outward mails for a whole year could not exceed 120 letters – and that was a very generous estimate – so consequently the provision of a mail service would be a complete waste of time and money.

Proof that St Kilda was not ready for a mail service was provided when the steamship *Mastiff* made her maiden voyage from Glasgow to Iceland in June 1878. Her owner was John Burns, later first Lord Inverclyde and founder of the Burns–Laird Line. The *Mastiff* was a vessel of 870 tons and 220hp, built for the Irish Royal Mail Service operated by Burns and his partner. Before entering regular service, the *Mastiff* set out from Castle Wemyss on the Firth of Clyde on the evening of 22 June, bound for Iceland, via St Kilda and the Faroe Islands.

In addition to Mr and Mrs John Burns with their sons James and George, the ship carried a number of friends, including Admirals Ryder and Farquhar and Captains Dennistoun and Colquhoun, RN. The commander of the vessel, however, was Captain William Kerr, who later entered the imperial Russian service and commanded the private yacht of the Czarina Maria Feodorovna. Among the civilian passengers were several society ladies, an Australian tycoon (Campbell Finlay) an ex-MP (Albert Grey) and the celebrated novelist Anthony Trollope, the 'chronicler' of the cruise and subsequently the author of a book entitled *How the 'Mastiffs' Went to Iceland*.

SS *Mastiff* at Castle Wemyss, from a sketch by Mrs Hugh Blackburn, forming the frontispiece of the very rare book *How the 'Mastiffs' Went to Iceland* by Anthony Trollope.

The *Mastiff* dressed overall at Reykjavik on her
maiden voyage, 1878 – a real photograph pasted
into each of the 100 copies of the book, published
privately for James Burns and his friends.

Trollope had had a glittering career in the postal service and took a special
interest in postal matters in the course of the voyage. One of the illustrations
in the book (from a sketch by Mrs H. Blackburn) showed John Burns standing
in the bows of the ship's longboat as it approached the landing place on St
Kilda. In his hand he held a small canvas bag containing the mail which had
been collected from the head post office in Glasgow and contained a solitary
letter. In the drawing can be seen six barefoot St Kilda men, clad uniformly in
Kilmarnock bonnets, waiting to haul the boat up on the rocks. Some distance
behind them are grouped their womenfolk and some children, but on the far
right can be seen the Rev. John Mackay, reminiscent of one of the characters
in Trollope's clerical sagas and a far cry from the Fagin-like caricature by Sands.
On Mackay's right was Emily MacLeod of MacLeod, 'of whose goodness in
going among them and remaining with them from time to time it is impossible
to speak in terms of too high praise'. Trollope continued: 'Charity can hardly go
beyond this, seeing that every hour of her presence is to them a blessing, and that
every hour of her presence there must be to her an exile.'

The following year the *Mastiff* paid a second visit to St Kilda and on that
occasion delivered a mailbag containing twenty-nine letters and 225 newspapers,
along with assorted book packets, on 29 May. It is recorded that a high proportion
of the newspapers were printed and addressed in Gaelic.

In his account of the maiden voyage Trollope devoted several pages to the
chapter on St Kilda and used all his narrative skills in describing the island:

Nothing can be more picturesque than the approach to St Kilda, seen as it was by us through
the rising fog. We came upon jutting rocks suddenly, as it were, to us who were uninitiated in
such matters. The captains and the mariners, no doubt, knew more about it, having felt their
way gradually through the darkened water. As we glided into the little bay by which the island
is approached, we saw arches in the rocks, through which the blue sea could be again seen,

John Burns (later first Lord Inverclyde) on the maiden voyage of the *Mastiff*, delivering the St Kilda mailbag, containing only one letter, 1878. Mrs Blackburn's somewhat idealised image of the St Kildans includes a rather genteel clergyman who would not have been out of place in one of fellow traveller Trollope's Barchester novels, but far removed from the reality of the Rev. John Mackay, the island's minister.

and the abodes of myriads of birds, which were disturbed by our steam whistle, and the sharp, serrated points of jagged cliffs, all so near us that every detail was clear to our eyes.

With his skills as a novelist and his long expertise as a postal surveyor, Trollope's account of St Kilda was much more factual and less opinionated than others penned in this period. After an objective survey of the island and its people, however, Trollope questioned their very existence. 'No region can be of real value, the products of which must be eked out by charity from other regions,' he wrote, summing up his well-reasoned arguments. However, he then added the rider:

Who shall say that these people ought to be deported from their homes and placed recklessly upon some point of the mainland? I have not the courage to say… But yet their existence cannot be good for them, and certainly not for their posterity; and as far as we can judge a time will come when that posterity must die out unless the people be removed. In the meantime it appeared to me that all is done for them that present kindness can do. And so the 'Mastiffs' having seen all that there was to be seen at St Kilda, went on upon their adventurous voyage.

Four

Rival Steamers

The *Dunara Castle* made a third excursion to St Kilda in June 1879; on this occasion Emily MacLeod travelled as a passenger both ways, only spending a few hours ashore. Perhaps word of her impending visit had reached the island, for the entire population, led by John Mackay, was lined up in its Sunday best to greet her when she landed. Having failed to secure the services of a nurse from the mainland and then having failed to recruit an island woman willing to learn English and travel south to be trained, Emily lowered her ambitions. She agreed with the minister that a female teacher was desirable and the main purpose of her flying visit was to select an islander for this purpose. She settled on Rachel Gillies, wife of Donald Ferguson, who was both the ruling elder and *baile maor* ('town officer' or village headman). Rachel was the mother of three remarkable boys who would all make their mark in the wider world: Alexander Gillies, who became a prosperous tweed merchant in Glasgow, Donald John, who became a Free Church minister, and Neil, who became postmaster of St Kilda in 1906 and held that appointment until the evacuation of the island. The lucrative prospect of an annual salary of £5, however, proved to be insufficient inducement.

The matter of a teacher dragged on for several years, but eventually it was resolved by the Edinburgh Ladies Committee of the Highland and Agricultural Society arranging for a young Free Church theological student to take a year out from his studies to serve as the island's dominie. This arrangement began in 1884 and continued for a number of years, putting the education of the St Kildans (both adults and children) on an excellent footing. It was also in this decade that Emily's ambition to provide a trained nurse finally bore fruit with the appointment of a widow, Mrs Ann MacKinlay, the first of a number of women who acted as midwives and brought to an end the scourge of infantile lockjaw which had resulted in the deaths of most newborn infants within days of their birth.

The well-publicised success of the *Dunara Castle* and her annual excursions to St Kilda inevitably tempted rival companies to organise their own trips. Martin Orme's chief rival in the coastal trade was John McCallum, who had his office at 62 Jamaica Street, in the heart of Glasgow, just around the corner from Orme's headquarters at 20 Robertson Street. Unlike Martin Orme, who resided outside Glasgow, Captain McCallum lived in a comfortable villa in Sedan Place, off Paisley Road, while his son and successor, John Junior, lived at 42 Hill Street, Garnethill, on the north side of Sauchiehall Street which, by the 1870s, was rapidly developing as Glasgow's premier shopping thoroughfare.

John Senior grew up in the age of steam navigation. This master mariner entered into a partnership with Andrew Ross who had been operating a small coastal freighter, the *Black Eagle*, since 1871. In February 1873 Andrew and his son, Andrew Mackenzie Ross, joined forces with McCallum to form the Western Isles Steam Packet Co., in which the latter had two shares. In this period they were also associated with William and Hugh Young, owners of the steam yacht *Nyanza* which visited St Kilda in that year.

This company began operations with a paddle steamer, built in 1860 for the Lusitania Steam Co. of Portugal, under whose flag she sailed with the name of *Lisboa*. She was a handsome ship, built by J. Reid & Co. of Port Glasgow, and re-boilered in 1873 by MacNab of Greenock. She was renamed *St Clair of the Isles*, which seems to suggest that she may have been intended for service in Orkney and Shetland. In fact she was confined to the Western Isles, instituting in July 1873 a weekly service from Glasgow on Thursdays to Dunvegan, Uig, Lochmaddy and Lochboisdale. On her maiden voyage, however, she broke down with engine failure while sailing down the Firth of Clyde, and limped into Campbeltown for repairs. Four weeks later she struck a reef in Loch Sunart and was badly holed, necessitating extensive repairs which lasted several months. Early in 1874 she was transferred to a new weekly run serving the little ports around Lough Swilly in Ireland, but later returned to the Western Isles route and operated in tandem with the 116 ton *Lady Ambrosine*, purchased by the company in 1874.

The Western Isles Steam Packet Co. offered both ships at auction in March 1875. *St Clair of the Isles* was bought by Harris & Goodwin of Birmingham and is believed to have ended her days in the East Indies, sailing under the Dutch flag. Her sister ship was purchased by John McCallum, who thereafter sailed her himself on the Hebridean service. Interestingly, from the outset, McCallum arranged his schedule to avoid clashing with that of Martin Orme, so that between them *Lady Ambrosine* and the *Dunara Castle* offered a regular twice-weekly service to the Western Isles.

McCallum's solo venture was evidently very successful, for he now commissioned a combined sail and screw steamer from Birrell of Dumbarton, launched on 13 April 1876 under the name *St Clair*. She had a gross tonnage of 136 and was powered by a compound two-cylinder engine by Walker, Henderson & Co. She entered the West Highland service in June that year. Every Monday she would leave her berth at the Kingston Dock on the south side of Glasgow with goods and passengers, calling at Greenock and departing from the Clyde at 4 p.m. She sailed through the Crinan Canal and called at the slate island of Easdale before going on to Oban, Tobermory (Mull), Salen on Loch Sunart in Morvern, and then across the Minch to Castlebay (Barra) and Lochboisdale (South Uist).

Given the treacherous nature of the west coast it is not surprising that this ship had her share of mishaps, but she seems to have been more than usually accident prone. On 20 June 1877 she ran aground in Loch Bracadale but she was successfully re-floated two weeks later. In September 1878, however, she ran aground at Salen in Loch Sunart and listed so badly that she filled with water. Eventually she was pumped out and re-floated, but on 26 October 1880 she was wrecked on a reef off Coll and sank.

During her brief career *St Clair* made two extended trips in June each year, calling at Rum, Colbost (Skye) and Locheport (North Uist), and in August 1879 she made her first excursion to St Kilda with a party of about two dozen ladies and gentlemen on board 'anxious to visit this now famous island'. On this occasion she left Glasgow on Thursday 4 August and arrived off Hirta at 8 a.m. the following Monday. She fired a cannon to signal her presence, then cautiously nosed her way into the bay where she dropped anchor about two hours later. A much smaller vessel than the *Dunara Castle*, she anchored closer to the shore, under the superintendence of John McCallum himself. An account of this visit, published in *The Highlander* of 22 August, observed sourly that the St Kildans offered hand-knitted goods and birds' eggs at twice the prices they were sold for in other parts of the Highlands, but that, of course, the novelty factor was an important consideration, and the tourists eagerly bought up the entire stock, amounting to about sixty pairs of stockings and fifty yards of homespun cloth. The ship weighed anchor at dusk and must have sailed straight home as she was back in Greenock by Wednesday afternoon.

John McCallum's handbill for sailings of the *St Clair* and *Lady Ambrosine*, June 1878.

The weather on this occasion had been excellent, but the following August, when the *St Clair* repeated the exercise, the weather was pretty foul and even the hardiest passenger found the voyage from Skye direct to St Kilda via the Sound of Harris 'very rough'. Captain McCallum and his crew, however, did everything in their power to make the trip enjoyable to 'most aboard'. The visit coincided with the deaths of two young St Kildans, and one of the passengers, the Rev. Mr Whitelaw of Kilmarnock, helped Mackay to officiate at the funerals. The anonymous correspondent who reported the visit for *The Highlander* (11 August 1880) noted that purchases of knitting and homespun cloth, including a quantity of ewe-milk cheese, amounted to about £30, a considerable sum.

McCallum's other vessel, the *Lady Ambrosine*, built in 1874, generally operated on a route which ran on Thursdays via Crinan, Easdale and Oban, but after Tobermory called at Croig on the north-west coast of Mull before heading for Coll and Tiree and thence to Barra and Lochboisdale. Although it has often been suggested that she, too, made occasional trips to St Kilda, there is no record of such having taken place.

In 1881 McCallum acquired a new ship, the *Hebridean*. With a gross tonnage of 330 she was twice the size of the *St Clair* but much smaller than the *Dunara Castle*. She was built by Thomas B. Seath at Rutherglen, a town upstream of Glasgow and not usually associated with shipbuilding, although Seath's yard actually turned out quite a number of ferry-boats, puffers and small coastal vessels. Her compound twin-cylinder engine was built by W. King & Co. She was a fine-looking ship and well-appointed and soon became a great favourite with tourists.

McCallum himself skippered her on her maiden voyage, a six-day excursion with St Kilda as the ultimate destination. Dr John Brydon, one of the passengers, subsequently wrote enthusiastically: 'With John McCallum & Co.'s splendid steamer *The Hebridean* the visit is rendered comparatively safe and certainly very pleasant. Without a doubt, the trip – John McCallum is both principal of the firm and captain – to St Kilda is the most enjoyable six days' sailing that can be found in the waters of the United Kingdom.' Flushed with the success of this venture, McCallum made at least one cruise to St Kilda a feature of his annual programme in subsequent years.

By this time McCallum had moved premises to 12 Ann Street, Glasgow, where he was officially described as 'Steamboat Agent' although he was also captain of the ship and unofficial postman, being entrusted with the mail for the manse and the 'schoolhouse' (the factor's house), where resided the young schoolmasters and also, from 1881, the island nurses. In that year Emily MacLeod secured the services of Mrs Ann Mackinlay (née MacLeod), a native of Skye who had

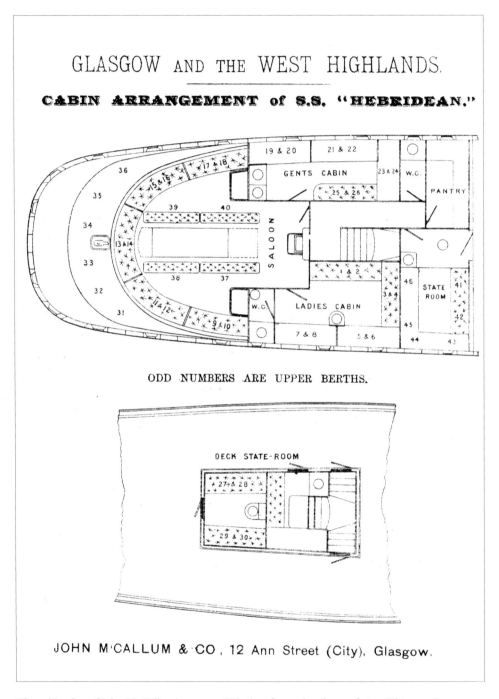

The cabin plan of John McCallum's steamer *Hebridean* from a brochure of 1890. This reveals a more spacious and better-appointed accommodation than that offered in her successor, the *Hebrides*.

acquired her diploma in midwifery in 1849 and would minister to the St Kildans until 1888, when she was well into her seventies. She died at Edinburgh three years later. Dr Brydon mentioned her as having the only ladies' bonnet on the island. During her first three years on the island she combined her nursing duties with that of teacher, prior to the appointment of Kenneth Campbell, the first of the theological students, in June 1884.

The cost of the round trip from Greenock to St Kilda by the *Hebridean* in the 1880s was 35s or 40s (£2), depending on whether you had a bunk in the saloon or a four-berth state room. In both cases the sleeping arrangements consisted of double-tiered bunks. In the saloon the seating by day became beds by night, with curtains tastefully screening off the double berths. McCallum seems to have been ahead of Orme in the production of a proper cruise brochure, which included diagrams of the 'cabin arrangement'. The ladies' cabin on the starboard side had eight berths, a washbasin and a water closet. On the port side there was a single toilet for the men but two wash basins and a total of thirty-eight berths, while the state room on the upper deck had four berths, a wash basin and a toilet adjoining at the top of the steps.

The route map of 1885 shows that the *Lady Ambrosine* was confined to the waters around the west coast, sailing from the Sound of Mull northwards to Muck, Eigg and Rum and thence to the little Skye ports of Carbost in Loch Bracadale, Dunvegan and Uig. The larger and more seaworthy *Hebridean* called at Coll and Scarinish in Tiree on the outward journey, then Castlebay (Barra), Lochboisdale and Carnan (South Uist), Scotvin off the south-eastern tip of Benbecula, Locheport and Lochmaddy (North Uist), Obbe in the Sound of Harris and then west to St Kilda. If the weather permitted, she then sailed north-east to Loch Roag on the west coast of Lewis before returning to the Sound of Harris and Uig, then proceeded southwards to Oban and Greenock. No wonder Dr Brydon enthused about such a splendid round trip. The cost was remarkably cheap, but the conveyance of tourists was incidental to the ship's main business of transporting freight, and there is no doubt that, between them, the *Dunara Castle* and the *Hebridean* performed an invaluable service to the isolated communities of the Inner and Outer Hebrides.

During the 1880s the rival companies settled into a routine whereby the *Dunara Castle* would visit St Kilda in June and the *Hebridean* in August. Although there was still the occasional chance visit of a private yacht, the two regular steamer visits provided the island's main contact with the outside world, yielding an annual income of £50 or £60, not to mention largesse which, although mainly in the form of sweets and tobacco, sometimes saw more substantial (and useful) articles provided.

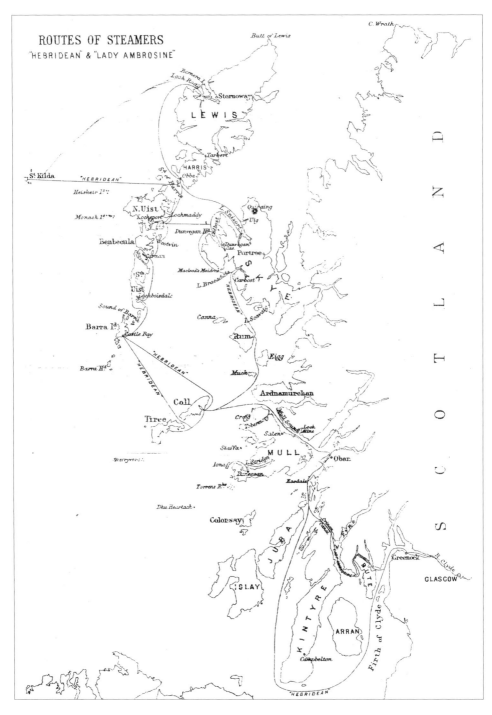

The steamer route map for the *Hebridean* and *Lady Ambrosine*, from McCallum's brochure of 1890.

During the period in which these ships made their annual visits, their movements were well-documented by the accounts which their more literary passengers invariably submitted to the press. In June 1880 the voyage of the *Dunara Castle* was chronicled by R. Scott Skirving of Edinburgh who had had his appetite for remote islands whetted by a previous visit to Foula in Shetland. On this trip he noted that, at Dunvegan, there came aboard Emily MacLeod – 'the grandest old Highland gentlewoman I ever met' – accompanied by her nephew Reginald (the future clan chief and the father of the redoubtable Dame Flora MacLeod). After a boisterous crossing in which even one of the ship's stewards succumbed to *mal de mer*, the *Dunara* entered Village Bay at 7 a.m.

Having yearned to visit St Kilda for some time – even to the extent of checking out the costs of chartering a private vessel for the purpose – Skirving wrote an account which reveals a great deal about his rather negative personality. He was unimpressed by the scenery and the birdlife, and extremely critical about the custom of doling out small gifts of sweets and tobacco, a practice he felt was unnecessary and should be stopped. Even the obligatory display of cragsmanship which invariably left other visitors spellbound only provoked a nasty remark about the St Kildans showing themselves 'to be quite civilized so far as the practise of extortion goes'. The islanders demanded *2s 6d* each for the fulmars they caught and Skirving noted smugly that they were eventually beaten down to sixpence. Then he whined: 'More senseless *ruffians* I never saw, as they kept swinging the dead birds about to the destruction of their plumage and seemed not to know that their *skins* were what was wanted. I wonder if they thought we were going to eat them.' The Rev. John Mackay was dismissed as 'the poor wretched specimen of a Free Church Minister' while the menfolk were roundly condemned as 'rude mercenary brutal Islanders'. He summed them up viciously: 'The inhabitants in everything save their rock exploits are as miserable a set of men as we may ever meet in Europe. Poor ignorant, ill–natured avaricious creatures unable to take advantage of the civilization now offered them. They are also the degraded slave of one of the most contemptible beings I ever saw – their *cretin* like minister…'

The *Dunara Castle* paid a second visit to St Kilda that year, calling at the end of August. In 1881 the ship just happened to be at anchor in Tarbert, Harris, on the very day the decennial census was taken. It shows that the ship had a crew of twenty-five, comprising five officers (master, mate, boatswain and two engineers), eight seamen, four firemen (stokers), four stewards and one stewardess, a cook, a clerk (purser) and a winch driver. The last–named was a

Dutchman and two of the stokers were from Ireland, probably Northern Ireland judging by their surnames. There were nine Lowlanders, mostly in and around Glasgow, and thirteen from the Highlands and Islands. Nine of the crew were from the Islands – three each from Skye and Tiree, two from Mull and one from Uist. The oldest member of the crew, a stoker, was fifty-six, while the youngest, one of the stewards, was only fourteen – the ship's boy.

One of the stewards was my great granduncle Charles McIntosh from Lower Ollach in the Braes, south of Portree. My grandfather's elder brother Charles was named after him and, in turn, he too went to sea, although nowadays he is better known as *Tearlach am Bard* (Charles the Poet), on account of his poems and bothy ballads.

There were only five passengers aboard that night, two female servants from Skye and the brother of one of them, a divinity student. The other passengers were a seaman from Uist and the Rev. Donald Nicolson, Free Church minister of Barvas in Lewis. Below is the relevant extract from the census:

Name	Marital Status	Age	Address	Occupation
Archibald McEwan	M	46	Craignish, Argyll	(Master)
Duncan Baxter	M	47	Colintraive, Argyll	(Mate)
Dugald McQuilkan	M	29	Kilcalmonel, Argyll	(Boatswain)
William Reid	M	44	Johnstone, Renfrewshire	(Chief Engineer)
William Galbraith	U	23	Stranraer, Wigtownshire	(2nd Engineer)
Malcolm McFadyen	W	36	Tiree, Argyll	(Seaman)
Donald Lamont	M	32	Kilmuir, Skye	(Seaman)
John McArthur	M	29	Iona, Argyll	(Seaman)
Alexander Campbell	M	29	Bunessan, Mull	(Seaman)
Norman McCaskill	M	32	Durinish, Skye	(Seaman)
Alexander McRae	M	34	South Uist	(Seaman)
Donald McFadyen	U	28	Tiree	(Seaman)
Donald McArthur	U	20	Tiree	(Seaman)
William Hazzeen	M	45	The Netherlands	(Winch Driver)
John Brown	M	56	Glasgow	(Fireman)
John Dunlop	M	28	Ireland	(Fireman)
William Beattie	M	25	Ireland	(Fireman)
John Brown	M	20	Kirkintilloch, Dunbartonshire	(Fireman)

Alexander Kay	M	44	Paisley, Renfrewshire	(Steward)
Charles McIntosh	U	22	Portree, Skye	(Steward)
Alexander Smart	U	19	Glasgow	(Steward)
Alexander Roberts	U	14	Port Glasgow, Renfrewshire	(Steward)
Agnes Donaldson	U	22	Glasgow	(Stewardess)
John McKinnon	U	25	Oban, Argyll	(Cook)
William Donald	M	38	Dalrymple, Ayrshire	(Clerk)
Angus MacLean	U	41	North Uist	(Seaman, Passenger)
Donald Nicolson	U	35	Barvas, Lewis	(Minister Free Church, Passenger)
Mary McCaskill	U	33	Durinish, Skye	(Servant, Passenger)
Ann Campbell	U	19	Durinish, Skye	(Servant, Passenger)
Malcolm C. Campbell	U	21	Durinish, Skye	(Divinity Student, Passenger)

Key to marital status: M – Married
U – Unmarried
W – Widower

It was apparently the *Dunara Castle* which took off the celebrated ornithologist and rock climber Richard M. Barrington. An Irishman, he had visited several of the remote islands off the west coast of Ireland including Great Blasket, the Irish counterpart to St Kilda (but not evacuated until 1953). He had arrived on the island three weeks previously when McCallum's new steamer *Hebridean* had called there. Reminiscing about his trip more than thirty years later Barrington was very hazy about how he got there. Writing to fellow naturalist J.A. Harvie Brown (July 1911) he mused: 'Don't I know the *Dunara Castle*, well, god bless me – is she alive still – for she took me to St Kilda 30 years ago – or from it – I forget which.' His memory was playing him false, for he then continued: 'Old David McBrayne was alive then – and offered to send her to St Kilda for me specially – if marooned – for £30 from Obbe.' But MacBrayne's steamers never went anywhere near St Kilda until some years later, and the *Dunara Castle* did not pass into the hands of that shipping line until after the Second World War. Barrington is now chiefly remembered for being the first 'outsider' to get to the top of Stac Biorach, the least accessible of all St Kilda's rocks.

Thereafter both the *Dunara Castle* and the *Hebridean* managed to pay two visits each to St Kilda in most years. In 1882 the *Hebridean* even made three trips and, with John Mackenzie going out in the spring and autumn in his own sailing boat, St Kilda was averaging six regular trips between the end of May and late August each year. Then (as now) there were times when the unpredictable weather in the Atlantic prevented the ships making a landing. Such was the case in June 1882 when the *Dunara Castle* entered the bay but had to leave hurriedly as a storm brewed up. The St Kildans launched their boat as usual and headed out to the steamer but almost capsized in the process and barely regained the shore. Not all voyages to St Kilda were plain sailing by any means; even in relatively calm weather – sea-sickness was a problem that sorely afflicted passengers and crew alike.

In the five years since the *Dunara Castle* first visited the island, the increasing frequency of steamer excursions had wrought socio-economic changes on St Kilda. Their new-found economic muscle freed the islanders from total dependence on MacLeod of MacLeod and his factor, both of whom, since the journalistic activities of John Sands, had been on the defensive to the world at large, though sometimes adopting bullying tactics with the people themselves. It was clear that the St Kildans, led by their wily minister, were acquiring skill in bargaining with the tourists. Writing to MacLeod in 1882, John Mackenzie complained that Mackay had become 'just as low, and as great a beggar as any of them', adding that the passengers aboard the *Dunara* were 'very much disgusted with him'.

A new-found stroppiness in their dealings with their proprietor and his factor was symptomatic of the wind of change then sweeping through the Highlands and Islands and doubtless the St Kildans were apprised of the rent strike and crofters' 'revolt' in Skye which eventually prompted the government to set up a Royal Commission of Inquiry. The commissioners, headed by Lord Napier, travelled all over the Highlands seeking evidence and taking statements from the people in each parish and, on Saturday 2 June 1883 they found themselves on St Kilda itself, having been transported from Tarbert, Harris, aboard HMS *Lively*, commanded by Captain Parr.

In his evidence to the commissioners Mackay had some trenchant comments about the tourists. When Lord Napier asked him if the steamers did any mischief by the sale of liquor or in any other way, the minister replied: 'Some of these passengers are very loose in their character, and some of them are drunk when they come ashore, but the people avoid them a far as they can.' When asked if these visits did any other harm, Mackay said that they were very annoying when they delivered tourists who stayed on the island through the Sabbath. When taxed about this, however, all he could complain about was the fact that 'they go about the hills, and go seeing through the windows and striking the dogs and one thing and another'.

Having taken evidence from Donald Macdonald and Angus Gillies, Lord Napier and his party concluded their enquiry and then set off to explore the island, watch the demonstration of cragsmanship, distribute the customary gifts and buy knitted goods and homespuns – just like any other tourists. HMS *Lively* weighed anchor at 9 p.m. and departed well before the commencement of the Sabbath. It was a fine evening and the commissioners were treated to a sail round the islands to admire the stupendous cliff scenery before heading back to Harris.

Although the pattern of sailings by the *Dunara Castle* and *Hebridean* was well established by 1884, in June of that year St Kilda had a visit from another private steam yacht, owned by Henry Evans, who apparently made several trips to the island in the 1880s. On this occasion he had on board an Inverness architect named Alexander Ross and a photographer from the same town, David Whyte, who gave a lecture the following winter to the Inverness Scientific and Field Club, illustrated with lantern slides. Later some of his images were published by him as postcards and are now much sought after. He seems to have sold the rights to some of his photographs to George Washington Wilson of Aberdeen. The glass negatives form part of the GWW collection in the library of Aberdeen University; originally prints were sold as tourist mementoes and then, after picture postcards were permitted in 1894, they became even more popular with visitors, versions being pirated by rival publishers for many years, including, rather confusingly, the firm of J.B. White of Dundee in the 1930s and David J. Whyte of the same city, leading to the suspicion that these postcard publishers were all related in some way.

Another passenger on this yacht was John MacWhirter, a celebrated landscape painter. Born in Edinburgh in 1839 he moved to London in 1867 and exhibited at the Royal Academy from 1865 to 1904, dying seven years later. He 'made some lovely drawings' according to the lecture given by Ross. Although MacWhirter produced some excellent landscapes of Perthshire, Skye and many parts of Europe and North America as a result of his extensive travels, his sketches of St Kilda have not been traced.

Earlier that month the *Dunara Castle* brought out Kenneth Campbell to begin his year as schoolmaster, while the visit of the *Hebridean* at the beginning of August brought the Misses Rainy and Blackie, respectively the daughters of the Free Church College principal and an eminent Edinburgh doctor, who bore with them 'a nice School desk' for the young teacher. Campbell left the island in June 1885, being replaced by Hugh McCallum, a Skyeman. He apparently travelled to St Kilda in John Mackenzie's smack.

A month later the *Dunara Castle* called on the last Monday of July 1885. One of the passengers on this occasion, R.A. Clarke, wrote an account of the voyage with particular reference to the visit to St Kilda which appeared in due course in the *North British Daily Mail* of 18 August. Clarke mentioned 'a native youth' who was reasonably proficient in English. This was clearly a reference to young

Alexander Gillies Ferguson, the ground officer's eldest son and the star pupil in the little school. Clarke wrote at some length about the rapidly acquired commercial acumen of the islanders. His article also contains one of the earliest references to the little copper brooches which the St Kildans cunningly fashioned out of a halfpenny and which they then sold to the tourists at sums ranging from 2*d* to 6*d*. After their demonstration of fowling, the men sold their catch to the highest bidders and several tourists returned to the ship with live puffins for which they had paid 6*d* or 1*s* each. What became of those poor birds one can only imagine. As for religious observance, Clarke also made a tantalisingly fleeting reference to a service described as 'the monthly Otter celebration' which was presumably a thanksgiving for the many kindnesses shown to them by Admiral Otter over the years.

John Mackenzie visited St Kilda in the *Robert Hadden* at the end of August, bringing out provisions which should have lasted until the following spring. Not long after that a Mr Cartwright had called at the island in his yacht *Firefly* and found everyone safe and well. But on Saturday 12 September St Kilda was ravaged by a severe storm which flattened the crops before they could be harvested, and inundated the store house, destroying the winter provisions and seed for next year's crop. In desperation, the islanders had recourse to 'mailboats' to communicate their plight to the outside world.

When I first met Alexander Gillies Ferguson in 1959 he claimed with some pride that it was he who invented the St Kilda mailboat, the method whereby the islanders relied on the wind and waves to get messages to the Western Isles, though occasionally they strayed farther and ended up in Orkney, Shetland, Iceland or Norway. Of course, we know that Lady Grange in the 1730s and John Sands in 1876 had used this method, but Ferguson was probably correct in asserting that he was the first St Kildan to employ it. His letter, addressed to his former schoolmaster Kenneth Campbell, was placed inside a medicine bottle and secured in the hull of a piece of wood roughly fashioned like a boat. Remarkably, it was recovered on Thursday 24 September on the beach near Gallan Point, a short distance from Aird Uig, where Campbell was now teaching.

The letter concluded cryptically: 'They send two boats from St Kilda to go to Harris not the fishing boats but little pieces of wood like the little one which I send'. This implies that the habit of sending 'mailboats' was not unknown to the islanders. In fact, two other mailboats were despatched about the same time, one containing letters from the minister to the Rev. Dr Robert Rainy (Principal of the Free Church Theological College) and the Rev. Alexander McColl of Lochalsh, recovered on the island of Taransay and handed over to the schoolmaster,

Alexander Sutherland who forwarded them with covering letters to the respective addressees. Mackay's letters said much the same thing, if more grammatically, but it was young Alexander's mailboat that turned up first and got the maximum publicity when the text was printed in the *Northern Chronicle* and soon copied by other newspapers, notably the *Inverness Courier*, which published Ferguson's letter along with a petition which the St Kildans had sent to Mr Balderston, the county assessor, setting out their grievances against their landlord.

John Mackenzie's initial reaction was understandably sceptical, and he was inclined to dismiss it as some boyish prank – 'I am surprised that a boy should be employed to despatch such an important message when there is a minister, a schoolmaster and a ground officer in the island to look after the interest and welfare of its inhabitants' – but he was nonetheless miffed that an appeal should have been addressed to outsiders rather than to himself.

Copies of the letters written by Ferguson and the minister were eventually forwarded to the Home Secretary in London, via Fletcher Menzies of the Highland and Agricultural Society to whom Dr Rainy had appealed. Rainy did not leave matters to the Government, assuming that they would act accordingly, but simultaneously consulted the well known Glasgow publisher, Sir William Collins. In a letter to Menzies, Rainy alluded to the publisher being 'extremely exact and businesslike' and intriguingly added that he 'knows the whole Hebrides, having been all round them in his own steam yacht', although there is unfortunately no record of Sir William ever having visited St Kilda. Nevertheless, it was thanks to his generosity that the steamer *Hebridean* was chartered by Collins at very short notice.

The *Hebridean* left Glasgow on the afternoon of Thursday 15 October with a cargo of seed corn, barley, meal and potatoes to the value of £110. At this late season she was not carrying passengers – save one, a Glasgow journalist, Robert Connell, who was despatched as a special correspondent for the *Glasgow Herald*. The passage of the relief ship attracted considerable attention at Oban and other ports where she called en route.

By Saturday night, she had only got as far as Lochboisdale. Before leaving Glasgow Captain McCallum had made it clear to Collins that he would only attempt the open Atlantic if the weather remained calm. Fortunately it had been 'mild and agreeable' up to that point. The ship left Lochboisdale at dawn on Sunday and reached Obbe by 11.30 a.m. Once she left the shelter of the Hebrides she encountered the open Atlantic, but luckily the wind was from the north-east. Although Connell experienced some discomfort during the 50-mile voyage over the open sea, he stated: 'notwithstanding the advanced period of the year the run… was never made under more favourable conditions. The sun shone out brilliantly all the time we were on the water; the wind, at first a little troublesome, moderated to a gentle breeze, and the swell of the mighty ocean, trying enough no doubt in all conscience to a landsman, was a mere ripple compared with what is often experienced in those seas.'

The *Hebridean* reached St Kilda about 4.30 p.m. Like many other visitors who arrived on the Sabbath, Connell was surprised to find the island apparently deserted. He then remembered what he had been told about the strict Sabbatarianism which kept them rigidly at their devotions, no matter how famished they might be. The ship steamed into Village Bay and anchored about 300 yards offshore. She blew her whistle, not only scattering the birds but also bringing some women out of their cottages. Although they seemed to be running around, no one came down to the shore to greet the ship, and all was silent in the church and manse. In one of many purple passages, Connell wrote of the minister: 'we had expected to see [him] in truly patriarchal fashion leading the way to the shore to bid us welcome, and convey through us the thanks of his flock to their kind benefactors.'

As no such procession was forthcoming, Captain McCallum ordered the lowering of the ship's boat. The skipper was accompanied by a Captain Alexander, 'from New Zealand', taking a busman's holiday. As it neared the shore the doors of the church opened and a stream of people ran down to the rocks to help the visitors disembark. The islanders gave them a very warm welcome, no doubt pleasantly surprised by a visit of the steamer at such an unlikely time of year:

> They pressed round about us in little knots quite as interesting from the picturesqueness of their dress as from the deep anxiety stamped upon every face, and insisted on being told in Gaelic, times without number, of the timely supplies on board the *Hebridean*, and of Sir William Collins, Dr Rainy and the other kind people in Glasgow and Edinburgh who had sent them.

Their excitement at the sudden appearance of the relief ship, after the worries and fears caused by the storm, was understandable. It later transpired that one of the woman fancied that she had heard gunfire the previous night and, communicating this to her husband and he to others, the islanders had got it into their heads that 'a Sassenach fleet had arrived off the coast to put them to the sword'. Connell sagely added: 'They were sufficiently wise in their generation to connect the fleet with the begging letters which they had sent on this and previous occasions.'

Predictably, Mackay would not permit the ship to offload her stores, although a few minutes after midnight the island boats were launched and the precious cargo brought ashore. By 3 a.m. this task was complete and the *Hebridean* weighed anchor, her return voyage to Glasgow being equally calm and uneventful.

In the meantime, the authorities had not been inactive. Instruction was made from London that Malcolm McNeill, Inspecting Officer of the Board of Supervision, should proceed at once to St Kilda and make an official report on the condition of its inhabitants. On this occasion the journey was made aboard the fishery cruiser HMS *Jackal*, now under Commander Osborne. On the afternoon of Tuesday 20 October, the ship left her base at Rothesay in the Isle of Bute. McNeill's report, published the following April, stated that the islanders 'were amply, indeed luxuriously, supplied' for the coming winter and that the stores brought by the *Hebridean* were more than sufficient. Although he conceded that conditions might be improved by the construction of a landing-place, on the whole he thought that it would be more economical in the long run to assist in the emigration of the inhabitants.

The delay in publishing McNeill's report did nothing to allay the concerns of the people on the mainland, who had been appalled at the alleged plight of the St Kildans. The *Glasgow Herald* decided to send Connell back there for a more detailed analysis of the situation. Rather than wait for the first steamer of the 1886 season, Connell travelled on the factor's schooner, *Robert Hadden*, on Tuesday 8 June. As well as the factor, John Mackenzie, the little ship had on board young George Murray, who was going out to replace Hugh McCallum as schoolmaster. While Kenneth Campbell and McCallum later became ministers of the Free Church, Murray became a full-time schoolteacher and eventually headmaster. He kept a diary which has been preserved, and which casts a fascinating light on St Kilda, especially on life during the long winter months when the island was virtually cut off from the outside world.

Connell described in laborious detail the voyage from Dunvegan by the little sailing ship. Although he did not say as much, he could not help contrasting the smooth voyage by steamer the previous October with the tortuous journey which, due to a total lack of wind, took them barely 2 miles in twelve hours. When they did reach the Sound of Harris, contrary currents retarded their progress still further. Eventually a fair wind got up and they reached their destination on Thursday morning. Connell was saddened to discover that the provisions brought by the *Hebridean* had only caused considerable strife due to discord over how they should be divided. So much for the 'primitive communism' allegedly practised on St Kilda!

Most of Connell's book, entitled *St Kilda and the St Kildians*, merely went over familiar ground and, though less vitriolic than Sands, he came to much the same conclusion regarding the minister. Indeed, due to his more moderate language, Connell's attack on the old man's character was probably much more effective. The final chapter addressed the future of St Kilda, and Connell was firmly in favour of emigration. The *Robert Hadden* had brought out the accumulated mails of eight months, amounting to just nine letters, of which six had been written by St Kildans who had immigrated to Australia in 1852. All had prospered and one even enclosed a sum of money to enable a young couple to go out there. When Connell returned to Dunvegan he carried a letter addressed to the Agent-General of Victoria in London, seeking assisted passages to Melbourne for three of St Kilda's able-bodied young men. Connell maintained that the St Kildans were almost unanimous in their wish to leave their island, the only dissent coming from 'one or two old men'. In the end, of course, the mood of the people swung back, and inertia prevented them taking such a momentous step.

Five

Alarums and Excursions

The *Hebridean* made her regular annual trip to St Kilda in July 1886 and this was duly recorded in the *Glasgow Herald* of 15 July. The name of the writer was not appended, but it appears to have been Robert Thomson of Kinning Park who, five years later, published a slim volume describing a trip to St Kilda which bears striking similarities in style and content. Published some years after his brief visit, Thomson indulged in the customary philosophical musings about the St Kildans and their character. Finding the island to be no utopia he concluded that it was 'one of the most miserable, lonely and desolate places in the British Isles', fit only as 'a Refuge for Inebriates, or a Convict Settlement'.

The newspaper report, coming hard on the heels of an article by Connell (28 June) added nothing new, although it seems clear that many of the other people on this particular excursion had been impelled to book passage as a result of reading Connell's article. By this time there was, in fact, a sort of self-fuelling situation, in that visits to St Kilda automatically resulted in press coverage which, in turn, encouraged further visits, with inevitable articles in the newspapers, no matter how repetitive they might be. The Rev. John Mackay, often facetiously styled the Bishop of St Kilda, got more press exposure than the Pope and the Archbishop of Canterbury together, though the pen portraits were often contradictory, depending on the bias and subjectivity of the writer. In this instance Mackay was dubbed the Mikado of St Kilda, in allusion to the Gilbert and Sullivan opera which was all the rage that year.

The only original note in this article concerned the skipper of the *Hebridean*, the redoubtable John McCallum. Contrary to Connell's description of Ann MacDonald (the minister's housekeeper) as 'the terror of the whole island', the writer found her to be 'not the tall virago I had pictured to myself' and went on to describe a fleeting visit to the manse, where he witnessed Ann plumping herself down on the gallant captain's lap as he 'playfully attempted to kiss her'. What the minister made of all this canoodling was not recorded.

Robert Thomson's book mentions the island's teacher. Although this young man was not actually named, the description fits George Murray, 'who had not been many weeks on the island, but who was wearying terribly already'. Homesickness and boredom were recurring notes in Murray's diary and the last entries before he finally departed give graphic evidence of the St Kilda equivalent of 'jail fever', as he railed at the non-arrival of the steamer. The *Dunara Castle* finally arrived on 7 June 1887, bringing Murray's replacement, Ranald MacDonald.

Captain McCallum was a great favourite with the St Kildans. Doubtless as the captain of his own ship he had more leeway than his counterpart on the *Dunara Castle* regarding steamer schedules, and could fit in additional trips to St Kilda as demand and opportunity arose, for he was a frequent visitor over many years. Significantly, it was to John McCallum rather than Martin Orme that the St Kildans turned in an emergency. In August 1887 Ranald MacDonald wrote to McCallum with the heart-breaking news that Annie, the daughter of Norman Gillies, had gone 'over the rocks' (the Hirta euphemism for falling off the cliffs). 'We thought she was dead,' he wrote, 'but life was in her. We took her home, and she is lying between life and death. I hope you will have a doctor on board the next time you come. The girl's head is badly cut and bruised. I wish you could bring something for healing.' McCallum immediately forwarded the letter to the *Glasgow Herald* which published it on 24 August.

On this occasion providence stepped in for, barely three days after the accident, the SS *Holly* of the Highland Fisheries Co. called at St Kilda, and among her passengers were several medical students. Two of them offered treatment but, inexplicably, this was turned down, and they had to be content with leaving instructions with the minister. Mackay was disgusted at the negative attitude of his parishioners but, as he had a medicine chest, he himself may have treated the girl, who apparently made a good recovery. Ann MacKinlay was still on Hirta at the time and would, in the normal course of events, have treated the injured lass. However, she was now very frail and elderly herself, and more of a liability than a help. A year later she officially retired to Skye, where she died in 1891.

An excursion to St Kilda aboard the *Dunara Castle*, which set out from Glasgow on 26 July 1888, was described at length by Dr Archibald Campbell in an article published in the *Oban Times* of 15 April 1889. It contained very little that was new, apart from the arrival of the latest nurse, Mrs Urquhart, complete with pet cockatoo, and merely repeated the now well-worn platitudes about the island and its inhabitants in general and the minister in particular. Less up-to-the-minute than the *Glasgow Herald*, perhaps, the *Oban Times* may have had Dr Campbell's article pending for some time, for it was overtaken by events some months before it appeared in print.

The most dramatic news from St Kilda, early in 1889, did not reach the outside world by steamship but by a 'mailboat', launched on 23 January that year and recovered by Murdo Mackay, Deputy Receiver of Wrecks, on the shore at Lower Barvas, Lewis, on 5 February. It was found to contain four letters, which had been badly waterlogged. After carefully drying them out, Murdo forwarded them to his superior, Mr Callender, at Stornoway. The letters were written on 22 and 23 January and were addressed to John Mackenzie, the factor at Dunvegan, the Rev. Murdo Mackenzie, Free North Church, Inverness, the Rev. Mr Urquhart of Stockport, Cheshire, and John Somerville of Renfrew Street, Glasgow. The letters revealed that the bulk of the congregation, led by Donald Ferguson, the ground officer and ruling elder, had seceded because Mackay had refused to baptise a child whose father was 'lying under Church discipline'.

The matter was aired in the *Inverness Courier* of 11 February under the headline 'Ecclesiastical Quarrel at St Kilda'. No fewer than sixteen of the nineteen families on the island had boycotted the church. The unsigned article observed: 'Having no true unit of measurement, it is the most natural thing in the world for small isolated communicates to lose sense of proportion, and to magnify their petty domestic squabbles into things of imagined world-wide importance.' This mini-Disruption had taken place in November 1888 and it was still rumbling on by the time the obligatory special correspondent for the *Glasgow Herald* was despatched on 4 April 1889 aboard the sailing vessel *Janet*, chartered from Peter McLean (the factor's little schooner *Robert Hadden* having been wrecked in Loch Dunvegan during a recent storm), to assess the situation for the wider world – for even the most trivial of storms in teacups on St Kilda were considered newsworthy.

The *Janet* reached St Kilda on the evening of Saturday 6 April, the newspaperman being greeted warmly by Murdo Macrae, the young schoolmaster who, with Mrs Urquhart, felt it politic to support the minister, along with his housekeeper Ann MacDonald and her brother Neil. The lengthy report, which appeared in the newspaper on 15 April, went into meticulous detail, presenting the pros and cons of the bitter argument. Several hundred words were expended on a sub-plot which concerned Mrs Urquhart's bonnet, the loss of which in a gust of wind had prevented her attending church – a matter which had mistakenly endeared her to the anti-minister faction for some time until, at the New Year, she had resolved to make a new hat and thus resumed her presence in the body of the kirk. The scenario, which was worthy of Trollope himself, was not lost on the newspapers, which likened the minister's housekeeper to Mrs Proudie. It was her tittle-tattling to the minister which laid the baby's father 'under scandal' and triggered off the dispute. By April 1889 the majority of the St Kildans would not be reconciled with the church until the wretched minister and his termagant housekeeper had been expelled. With remarkable even-handedness the journalist offered both sides of the argument, and recited in full the allegations of Mackay, accusing Donald Ferguson of continually undermining his authority.

The matter was tedious in the extreme, but no doubt the report gave the sophisticated readers of the *Glasgow Herald* a good laugh. The Free Church, however, took a dim view of this unseemly conduct and, within twenty-four hours of the report, its Highlands Committee had met and resolved to sack Mackay. In due course the Rev. Angus Fiddes of Portmahomack, Easter Ross, was selected as a replacement.

With St Kilda back in the news again, albeit for all the wrong reasons, there was quite a flurry of steamer activity that summer. First on the scene was a newcomer, at least so far as St Kilda was concerned. This was the *Clydesdale* of about 450 tons. She had been built in the spring of 1862 by J.&G. Thomson for the firm of David Hutcheson & Co. Hutcheson and his brother Alexander had been senior employees of George & James Burns who, on relinquishing their interests in the coastal trade in February 1851 to expand their transatlantic business, had handed over to the Hutcheson brothers, whose junior partner was a nephew of Messrs Burns, by the name of David MacBrayne. When the Hutcheson brothers retired, MacBrayne became sole partner, and changed the company name in 1879.

The *Clydesdale* was originally fitted with inverted-cylinder, surface-condensing engines, but was re-boilered in 1869, and again in 1893 when she acquired two funnels in place of the original one. She was mainly used on the Glasgow–Stornoway route but, after MacBrayne acquired the *Claymore* in 1881, the older ship was relegated to a relief capacity. From 1889 onwards she was employed on the run from Oban to the more southerly of the Outer Hebrides, and thus she was available for the special trip to St Kilda which took place in June 1889 under Captain MacEachnie – 'a thorough master of the difficult navigation of the Island Route', as the *Oban Times* assured its readers on 25 May.

Although this photograph purports to show the *Dunara Castle* at Village Bay, in around 1900, it is probably the steamer *Clydesdale* in the 1880s, judging by her rakish bows. The *Dunara Castle* had a more vertical bow profile.

In fact, the *Dunara Castle* called at St Kilda on 6 June, not only with the usual complement of tourists on board but also three ministers of the Free Church who had been sent thither for the express purpose of checking the situation for themselves as well as giving Mackay his marching orders. He was offered a pension of £40 per annum – half his annual stipend – to retire. At first he tried to squeeze another £10 a year out of them but the deal was not negotiable. Bowing to the inevitable, the elderly minister then told them he intended leaving St Kilda at the earliest opportunity. The Free Church delegation spent four days on the island and then left on the *Clydesdale*, whose forty passengers swarmed all over the village, anxious for a sight of the dreaded Ann Macdonald and the poor old minister, who prudently took to his bed. When the *Hebridean* called on 26 June, Mackay and his loyal housekeeper went on board. Mackay's parting shot to young John Ross as he went up the gangway was a masterpiece of understatement: 'I think it is time I was leaving them now.'

When the *Hebridean* reached Lochmaddy the following day no fewer than nine persons from St Kilda disembarked, according to the *Oban Times* of 6 July. As well as the minister and his housekeeper, they included (according to the newspaper) Mackay's sister and nephew, along with a girl, Mary MacQueen, accompanied by her aunt and uncle, Christina and Neil MacKinnon, and Mr and Mrs Ewan Gillies. The MacKinnon party intended crossing to Skye to consult a physician there about suspected cancer in the young girl, but Ewan Gillies was a restless individual who had gone to Australia and then California, before returning to St Kilda to unsettle everyone with his bragging of the big, wide world, and who was now planning to return to America for good.

There seems to have been some confusion here for Mackay's sister, Margaret, who had originally kept house for him. She died in 1878, according to her tombstone in the tiny circular cemetery. It seems more likely that the sister and nephew were Ann Macdonald and her kinsman, nineteen-year-old John Ross Macdonald, who had lived with her in the manse and was employed as a handyman. For some years the elderly minister lived in a cottage opposite the hotel in Dunvegan, but in 1895 he moved to Kilmuir, and a year later returned to his native village of Jeantown, Lochcarron, where he died in April 1901.

When the *Hebridean* paid another visit to St Kilda on 12 August that year she had aboard a party of tourists from Stirling, including two ministers and two bailies, as well as David W. Logie, who had literary pretensions that found expression in the pages of the *Stirling Sentinel*. His account of the voyage was published in two consecutive weekly numbers. Aboard ship were the MacKinnons and Mary MacQueen, returning from their sojourn in Skye. The girl had been sent to Edinburgh for treatment in a hospital there but, after several weeks, had apparently been pronounced fit, or at least well enough to return to St Kilda.

Logie must have possessed extraordinary powers of perception – certainly he would have put Sherlock Holmes in the shade. In the first of his two articles he described the two women he encountered aboard ship: 'They were of medium height, and seemed intelligent, though evidently lazy, and of a dependent and sneaking nature. It was somewhat difficult to keep up a conversation with them...' A total ignorance of a language which the Lowland Scot dismissed as nonsensical babbling must have been some handicap in Logie's assessment of the character of the two women. The laziness and sneakiness which he was so quick to detect may have been no more than the hesitancy of people trying to converse in a language that was unfamiliar to them. But on such subjective spurs of the moment did so many self-proclaimed authorities pontificate about St Kilda in the press.

When they anchored for the night at Locheport the St Kildans sang Gaelic psalms, which Logie patronisingly described as having 'really a charming effect – an effect which, in its quaintness, no music in any church could equal'. Not to be outdone, of course, a party of English tourists Logie took care to name individually 'entertained the company with song and recitation'. On landing at St Kilda he noted the effusive greetings of kith and kin for the returning trio – 'the flow of gibberish was something overpowering'. There was the customary poking around in the cottages along the street, then interviews with the new incumbent at the manse and a lightning assessment of the young schoolmaster John Ross, who Logie misnamed as Macfarlane in his article.

At least Logie showed some originality in his purchases. Disappointed that he could not buy a wren (which was out of season) he settled on a pair of live fulmars. On the homeward voyage one of the birds got tangled in the string tethering it to the bed post and strangled itself. Logie kept the other bird occupied with morsels of raw fish, repaying his hospitality by doing what fulmars do best – squirting oil at all and sundry. The fulmar has been dubbed the skunk of the bird world with some justification, for the stench is not only overpowering but virtually impossible to eradicate. Amazingly, Logie described this episode in the local newspaper, oblivious to what a total ass he had made of himself.

What John Ross made of this buffoon may be gleaned obliquely from an entry in his diary shortly after this visit: 'One can have no idea of a St Kildan by paying him a flying visit… And the way he treats a stranger depends greatly on the stranger himself. What else could one expect from the inhabitants of such an isolated island?' His tenure as schoolmaster ended on 31 August 1889 when he departed on the *Clydesdale*, making her second trip of that year. He was therefore not around to witness one of the most remarkable of all the visits made by a steamer to the island.

During his fleeting visit in 1886, Robert Thomson's guide round the village was Ann Ferguson, the eldest child of Donald Ferguson and his wife Rachel. Tall, handsome and above average intelligence, like her brothers, Ann emerged as the uncrowned Queen of St Kilda, certainly after the departure of the Rev. John Mackay and his housekeeper in the summer of 1889. In the period of the 'vacant see' before another minister could be appointed, Donald Ferguson consolidated his dominant position. Mackay's replacement, Angus Fiddes, aged forty-seven, was not only a much younger man but also an infinitely wiser one.

No doubt he had been apprised of recent events on the island and, soon after his arrival, he secured the services of elderly Catherine MacLennan from Carloway in the west of Lewis, who may have been a minister's servant elsewhere previously. Fiddes soon acclimatised himself to the ways of his remote parish. Unlike his predecessor, he would take regular holidays on the mainland, although invariably using these trips to improve his knowledge of medical matters in general and midwifery in particular. If the island women persisted in their unsanitary ways, heedless of the advice given by the nurses, they were more inclined to listen to the advice given by a man of the cloth, from a pulpit that was said to be the loftiest anywhere in the Highlands. Energetic and open-minded, Fiddes even joined the St Kildans in their expeditions to Boreray and Soay, and earned their respect the hard way.

That he was a man of high intelligence and diplomacy is also revealed by his handling of a rather delicate situation that arose in the autumn of 1889. A few months earlier, John Ross had been contacted by James Gall Campbell, a Scotsman who had become successful in business in Sunderland and owned the local newspaper, the *Daily Echo*. Campbell was a brash individual, something of an entrepreneur, and he had a flair for showmanship. Organised tourism was still in its infancy but it appears that Campbell had already organised a number of excursions to the West Highlands with some success. By the time of his death in 1902 he had apparently organised almost seventy of these tours and was well regarded in Oban (especially at the Balmoral Hotel where his parties were invariably accommodated). As far as can be ascertained, he had never set foot on St Kilda, but he saw that, by the late nineteenth century, it was rapidly becoming the ultima Thule of the Victorian tourist.

Until this time, he had contented himself with reading all about it and vicariously playing the benefactor. Campbell had sent bags of marbles for the boys and later a consignment of books, hoping for a selection of birds' eggs in exchange. But now his ambition was to get much more closely involved. Indeed, he aimed to play a central role in a little drama which would surely grab the headlines. Campbell planned to visit St Kilda the following summer and, having got wind of the impending nuptials of Ann Ferguson and the island's only eligible bachelor, her cousin John Gillies, he got it into his head to organise the event. With his entrepreneurial flair in overdrive, Campbell decided that it would be great fun to organise an excursion to St Kilda, so that the civilised world could enjoy the spectacle of an island wedding. Ann and her beau would have been married in the autumn of 1889 without any fuss, but apparently there was a snag – Fiddes, though a minister, had not been ordained (the ecclesiastical laying on of hands did not take place till 1890), and therefore he was not competent to carry out a marriage. The young couple therefore determined to travel all the way to Glasgow by the first steamer of 1890 to tie the knot.

Although John Ross had left the island in the autumn of 1889 and settled in at Kingsburgh, Skye, with his sister as housekeeper, he continued to act as the go-between in this extraordinary affair and even agreed to join Campbell's party when it journeyed to St Kilda in May 1890. Over the intervening months he was privy to Campbell's plans which included providing the bride's trousseau and a new suit for the groom, as it would have looked very odd if he turned up at the ceremony in his everyday homespuns. Simultaneously Campbell was amassing a veritable mountain of wedding presents, including a huge consignment of books of all kinds and an astonishing range of consumer goods which he may have persuaded the manufacturers to donate in the hope of gaining some useful publicity from the stunt.

The correspondence between Ross and Campbell has survived and suggests that the young schoolmaster naïvely went along with Campbell's harebrained scheme because he saw the exercise as a means of dragging St Kilda into the civilised world. Angus Fiddes apparently only learned of the project from the *Oban Times*, and immediately voiced his concerns to Mrs MacLeod of MacLeod in a letter written only four days before the ship was due to arrive. 'I have grave doubts as the sincerity of his motives', he wrote, 'All this is being for mercenary purposes, the gratification or amusement of his party... in the first place to give sport to his party at the expense of the simplicity of the people and secondly to publish a record of the event and other things he can gather together and colour the materials with truth and falsehoods in such a taking manner as will command a ready sale in the market.'

Fiddes had done everything in his power to warn the St Kildans as well as apprise the Moderator of the Presbytery, the Rev. John MacLean of Tarbert, Harris. Doubtless he had also been praying for storms or at least a contrary wind, but the weather was continuing unseasonably calm. As for the 400 books which Campbell had promised, Fiddes pointed out that the island was already quite well stocked with the usual Gaelic literature, even if these books were now rather dog-eared and suffering from the very damp climate: 'It is simple folly bringing so many [books] here to rot upon one another with damp.'

On 27 May the *Clydesdale* left Oban with the Campbells on board. In the ship's hold reposed a vast quantity of goods which included a wedding cake of gigantic proportions as well as a harmonium or American organ. The cake, at least, was edible, but what the St Kildans thought of the 'Devil's kist of whistles' can only be imagined – the Free Church regarded music that did not come from the human voice as anathema.

The following afternoon the ship, gaily dressed over-all and blasting its steam whistle, anchored in Village Bay. Campbell, with a large party of wedding guests, about fifty in number, who had paid handsomely for the privilege, eagerly scanned the shore for the throng of jubilant islanders there to greet them. At first they were rather disappointed that there did not appear to be the enthusiastic reception generally accorded visiting steamers. At length a boat put out from the shore and presently there came aboard Donald Ferguson with his son Alexander as interpreter. Immediately Alexander (later described as 'an intelligent and well-educated youth') addressed Campbell in no uncertain terms. His sister was not going to be married that day and there would be no wedding.

Campbell was not a man to be rebuffed easily. Hastily summoning a minister named Rae whom he had hired to perform the ceremony, along with John Ross who had joined the party at Lochboisdale, and a gaggle of reporters and photographers in tow, they got into one of the ship's boats and rowed ashore. By now, the islanders were on the rocks to meet them, hand-knitted goods and birds' eggs ready for immediate sale. Among the islanders was Ann Ferguson herself, who Campbell accosted, flashing an array of wedding rings. She was eventually persuaded to try them for size while her fiancé looked on impassively 'at the arrangements that were being made for his happiness'.

Undeterred by this lack of response, Campbell and his cohorts proceeded to the manse. Fiddes received them politely but with dignified negativity. Campbell's patience was beginning to wear thin and he testily asked Fiddes why there would be no wedding. The latter replied that he was only a missionary and that it was a matter for the Rev. John MacLean, minister of Harris in which parish St Kilda nominally lay. In fact, Mr MacLean might be coming out to St Kilda the following month and the wedding might take place then. Fiddes brought the meeting to a close by politely thanking Campbell for the books. While Campbell retired discomfited, Fiddes mollified the press boys by giving them the potted tour of the village and proudly showing off his little garden. The special correspondent for *The Scotsman* provided the fullest account of the fiasco for his newspaper's 30 May edition.

By now the excursionists, described by the journalist as 'North of England Whitsuntide holiday-makers', had been ferried ashore and had learned that there would be no wedding after all. Making the best of a bad job they enjoyed the warm, mild evening by doing what all the other tourists did, wandering through the village, poking their noses into open doorways, or kicking the dogs that swarmed like a wolf-pack, before clambering up the steep slopes for the standard display of cragsmanship. Sweeties and tobacco were duly distributed, and purchases of island wares preceded the return to the relative comfort of the ship. Some St Kildans accompanied them in order to goggle at the extraordinary array of wedding presents, which included a silver teapot and matching teaspoons specially engraved for 'the Queen of St Kilda', as well as two dozen microscopes, three dozen pairs of spectacles, feeding bottles, paint boxes, and a dazzling assortment of branded goods (which Campbell hoped 'the Queen' would endorse for the purpose of advertisements), including 'Bovril meat extract, cough syrups, ointments, pills, magic cleansers, hair restorers and corn cures'. *The Scotsman* reported that the wedding presents amounted to over seven hundredweight.

Most of this cargo appears to have returned to Oban with the tour group, and Campbell then had the uncongenial task of returning everything to the donors. But the crates of books were unceremoniously dumped on the rocks above the landing place, and there they lay until the wind and rain and the spring tides removed them. Campbell tried to save face by asserting that the wedding had been aborted by the bride's father as he did not wish to lose his daughter, but it was a feeble excuse which fooled no one.

Six

Turn of the Century

From 1890 onwards both McCallum and Orme seem to have averaged two trips each to St Kilda in the brief summer period. Apart from the tourists, most of whom came and went without leaving any tangible record, there were naturalists and writers. In June 1896, for example, the *Dunara Castle* brought out the brothers Richard and Cherry Kearton, whose book, *With Nature and a Camera* (published by Cassells in 1897), devoted almost 200 pages to their sojourn on the island. They noted that, six years after the wedding fiasco, the rotting books dumped by Campbell still littered the landing place. The Keartons from the Home Counties were accompanied by John T. Mackenzie, son of the factor, who ensured that they were made comfortable in rooms of the factor's house. They were accompanied by another naturalist, John Young. The *Dunara* also had on board young Alexander Ferguson, returning for a summer break from his employment with a commercial firm in Glasgow. He had left St Kilda in 1894 to gain experience of buying and selling tweed cloth and other products of the Highlands and Islands and, before the century was out, would be in business on his own account, with premises at 93 Hope Street in the city centre.

The greater frequency of the tourist steamers also enabled mainland bureaucracy to extend its tentacles to a remote island which had hitherto been ignored. On this occasion, the *Dunara* conveyed from Obbe a Mr Strachan, sub-inspector of schools for Inverness-shire, who closely examined the school conducted by Fiddes and an 'assistant student', George Matheson from Harris.

The *Dunara* in Village Bay about 1900, unloading stores over the rocks before the jetty was built two years later. While the men manhandle their boat up on to the rocks at the Point of Coll, one of the St Kilda women can be seen in the foreground, bent double under a heavy sack.

Strachan confided the results of his examination to the Keartons who duly recorded in their book that there were concerns that some parents had absented their children and seemed to have little interest in their education.

In August that year the *Hebridean* visited St Kilda. On 12 August it anchored at Dunvegan where it was learned that Emily MacLeod of MacLeod had died three days earlier at the advanced age of eighty-five. An anonymous passenger subsequently submitted an article entitled 'The Hebrides and St Kilda' to the *Dalkeith Advertiser* where it was published in two parts (1 and 8 October). This account added little to what had endlessly appeared in print, although it was recorded that, as the steamer crossed the Minch, the ship's purser sang 'Over the Sea to Skye', with the assembled passengers joining in the chorus. Shortly before the *Hebridean* left St Kilda on this occasion Fiddes, accompanied by a man and woman who were his guests at the manse, came aboard, and the minister made a touching address to the passengers about his life and work on the island. The sincerity of his sense of vocation touched his audience deeply.

Unloading stores on the rocks, from photographs by Norman Heathcote in 1899. The barrels would have contained fulmar oil. Note the use of planks as an improvised landing stage in the period that immediately preceded the construction of the jetty in 1902.

On Saturday 11 June 1898 the *Dunara Castle* brought out a stonemason by the name of Macdonald, in charge of ten men who had been sent thither to erect the little school attached to the rear of the church. They spent three months on the island, carrying out extensive repairs to the church at the same time. The large quantity of timber, roofing materials, machinery and other stores were ferried ashore by means of a hastily improvised raft, a perilous undertaking due to the swell which rose and fell against the rocky landing place. As midnight approached, the task was only half-completed, but the islanders refused to help on account of the impending Sabbath 'and got perfectly frantic at the bare suggestion that they should'. Such ingratitude was hard to tolerate but, with long experience, the skipper should have known better than to attempt such a complicated task on a Saturday. Macdonald and his workmen were compelled to carry on right through the night and it was not until 4 a.m. on Sunday that all the stores were safely ashore. The men fell asleep, exhausted, in the open air, but fortunately it was already dawn on another warm, sunny day. Thereafter they were billeted on the island.

On this occasion the *Dunara* also brought out two gentlemen by the name of Robertson (unrelated), one a school inspector and the other the medical officer of South Harris, who had come to assess the educational attainments of the children and vaccinate them. John T. Mackenzie was also on board and remained on the island for about two weeks, awaiting the next visit of a ship to return to Skye. With him he had a young couple, the brother and sister Norman and Evelyn Heathcote. They were related to the MacLeods of MacLeod and planned to spend ten days on the island, lodging at the factor's house. Evelyn performed the ceremony of laying the foundation stone for the school, interring a sweetie jar containing a recent newspaper and a document signed by all the male inhabitants (though John Mackenzie had to forge the signatures of the illiterates). The Heathcotes returned the following summer and their experiences were distilled into a charming book, simply entitled *St Kilda*, published by Longman in 1900. Norman Heathcote was an accomplished watercolourist and an excellent photographer, and his book was beautifully illustrated as a result. A photograph on page 35 showed the arrival of the steamer, the *Dunara Castle*, lying at anchor in front of a fog-bound Dùn, while several men can be seen in the foreground, manhandling huge barrels over the rocks at the landing place.

The various schemes for creating a proper landing place had been mooted for four decades, but at long last something positive was being done about the problem. In June and July 1898 Fiddes spent a large part of his summer vacation on the mainland raising the matter of providing some sort of docking facility. He lobbied everyone who might have some influence on the matter and received a generally positive response, so much so that when he returned to St Kilda he was confident that 'next year's visitors will be landed at a pier'. He should have been on the island long enough to realise that a pier, by its very nature, would be destroyed at the first south-easterly storm. Something very much more substantial would have to be provided.

The project was eventually prompted by the possibility that St Kilda might become a fishing station. The Congested Districts Board (instituted in 1897) commissioned a survey from its resident engineer, Captain Andrews, and, in June 1899, he visited the island with the MacLeod of MacLeod to study the problem. He concluded that the only viable solution was to create a small dock protected by a stout wall, with a ramp up which the St Kildans could haul their boats by means of a winch. The boulders cleared from the dock area could be used in constructing the jetty. Colonel J. Gore Booth, consulting engineer to the Secretary of State for Scotland, recommended that 'a Supervisor experienced in such work and accustomed to the use of explosives' should be appointed at a weekly salary of £3 to oversee the work carried out by the St Kildans themselves 'at fair wages'. Gore Booth's report also suggested that the supervisor might communicate with the lighthouse on the Monach Islands, 35 miles due east, by lamp, using the Morse code – the first instance of some form of telegraphic contact.

The estimated cost of the work was originally set at £1,000 and this inevitably raised the question of whether it might not be cheaper in the long run to evacuate the island and resettle the inhabitants in Skye or the colonies. In the end the cost was reduced to about £600 and the vexed question of evacuation was again put off. Consequently Walter E. Wookey and his assistant, Edward Matthews, were hired to supervise the work. Wookey with Mr and Mrs Matthews travelled on the *Hebridean* from Glasgow in August 1899 with a vast amount of stores and provisions to see them through the long winter. Disembarking on 19 August, they put up at the factor's house with Mrs Matthews acting as cook-housekeeper. Wookey recruited seventeen men to do the heavy work, and five boys to assist in transporting the stores over the rocks from the landing place. The work continued right through the winter, although from November onwards the working hours were reduced by the poor light. It proved to be a labour of Sisyphus, with periodic storms hurling huge boulders back into the docking area whence they had so laboriously been removed.

Norman Heathcote alluded to this project in his book:

> The violence of the winter storms precludes the possibility of building a breakwater, and it
> has been determined that the only feasible plan is to blast an L-shaped passage in the rock
> where the boats will find shelter in moderate weather, and where it will be possible to land
> goods on many days when it would be out of the question under existing circumstances.

And in a footnote, written while the book was going through the press, he added
that, when the *Dunara Castle* made her first trip at the beginning of June 1900,
'the new shelter enabled them to land goods and passengers in spite of a south-
easterly gale'. The bulk of the work was completed by that time and Wookey
and the Matthews left on the *Dunara* at that time, arriving back in Greenock on
27 June. Work resumed in May 1901 (though why there was such a long gap is
not explained) and the project was completed in August. Too short and rock-
bound, it never permitted ships actually to tie up alongside, although it made
the landing of passengers and stores from small boats infinitely less hazardous
than before.

In April 1898 the *Hebridean* was replaced by the *Hebrides*, and she made her
first voyage to St Kilda towards the end of July that year. It was on a subsequent
trip by this ship that the Heathcotes returned to St Kilda in 1899. Referring to
this, Norman wrote:

> I was sorry to see the captain of the *Hebrides* forcing whisky on the crew of the native boat.
> They obviously did not want it. When he handed them down a glass, each man took a sip
> and passed it to his neighbour, but he kept giving them glass after glass, and though most of
> them refused to have any more, one or two of the weaker-minded men drank it, and were
> certainly none the better for it.

Tipped into each book opposite this page was an erratum slip in which Heathcote
recanted: 'I find that I was mistaken in saying that the present Captain of the
Hebrides gave whisky to the St Kildans, and I desire to apologise for my mistake.'

This vessel was constructed by the Ailsa Ship Building Co. of Troon on the
Firth of Clyde. She was 180ft in length and had a gross tonnage of 585, making
her much larger than her predecessor. Her triple-expansion engines were built by
G.L. Watson, producing an average speed in excess of 12 knots. She was purchased
by John McCallum & Co. as a successor to the *Quiraing* which, in turn, had been
acquired in 1890 as a successor to *Lady Ambrosine*. *Quiraing* had a varied career,
having been built in 1870 for the Ardrossan Shipping Co. and originally named

Landing stores at the jetty. This was one of a series of postcards published in 1919 by Alexander Gillies Ferguson and reprinted in several different versions. It shows the jetty erected in 1902, a vast improvement over the rocky landing place traditionally used.

South Western. Thirteen years later she was sold to Gustaf Gollcher of Malta and sailed in the Mediterranean under the name of *La Vallette* (one of the most famous of the Grand Masters of the Knights of St John) for seven years before being sold to John McCallum. She operated on the Glasgow–Iceland route but was disposed of in August 1896 to the Ayr Steam Shipping Co. and renamed *Merrick*. About 1899 she was sold to McDowell and Barbour of Piraeus and, under her fifth name, *Clio*, she sailed the Aegean until she was wrecked in 1904. Such a varied history and frequent change of name were not uncommon at that period.

The *Hebridean* remained with McCallum as a reserve ship, being occasionally chartered out to other companies, and for several years employed on the West Highland route during the quiet winter months. In May 1917 she was sold to Peter S. Cooper of Kirkwall and renamed the *Express*. Under her new name, however, she had a very brief career, sinking on 9 February 1918.

The first ship by the name of *Hebrides* was the pride and joy of the West Highland trade and put John McCallum ahead of his rival Martin Orme, who continued to operate with the *Dunara Castle*. In the early 1890s the General Post Office awarded the two companies an annual payment of £500 between them

No. of Manifest.

Telegraphic Address—' M'CALLUM," Glasgow.
Cor. Telephone No. 2193.
Nat. „ „ 7402. 93 ARGYLE

10 ANN STREET (City),

37

Glasgow, 4/St. 12/ 190

Mr J Y McKenzie Dunvegan

To JOHN M'CALLUM & CO.

For FREIGHT to . WEST HIGHLANDS per Steam-Packet "Hebrides" or "Hebridean."

For Conditions of Carriage see back hereof.

GOODS.	SENDER OR CONSIGNEE.	RATE.	AMOUNT
July 25 1 box, 1 Truss, 1 Hhr Dunvegan to St Kilda			
1 " Bread		250	5 -
Aug 14 1 bdle Skins			
1 bag Wool Soay to Carbost 256			1 -
1 Fish box			
4 ety casks			
1 pcl Glass, 1 tin			
Paint 2 bdles wood Ground Officer St Kilda ,			9 4
„ 29 1 bag Wool Y McQueen		260	2 -
1 box, 1 bdle Hoops Ferguson	„	„	2 -
		£ 1 . 6

Received payment.
30th December 1903
John M'Callum & Co.

An invoice from John McCallum, dated 4 December 1903, to John Mackenzie of Dunvegan, itemising freight conveyed to St Kilda by the steamers *Hebridean* or *Hebrides* in the previous July and August. The entry for goods carried from Soay refers to the island off Skye and not the St Kildan island of the same name.

Manifest No.

TELEGRAPHIC ADDRESS: "M'CALLUM," GLASGOW. | COR. TELEPHONE No. 2193.
NAT. „ „ 93 ARGYLE.

36 OSWALD STREET,

Glasgow, 31 / 10 / 190 3

Mr J S McKenzie Dunvegan

To JOHN M'CALLUM & CO.,

For FREIGHT from WEST HIGHLANDS, per Steam-Packet "HEBRIDES" or "HEBRIDEAN."
FOR CONDITIONS OF CARRIAGE SEE BACK HEREOF).

3 /

MARKS & NOS.	GOODS.			Weight or Measurement.	RATE.	AMOUNT.
July 26	1 Truss 1 Hhr					
Aug 15	1 box Bread 1 box	Dunvegan to St Kilda		250	.	5
	1 bdle Skins					
" 29	1 bag wool	M'Leod of M'Leod Cartool		256	.	1 6
	1 " "	S M'Queen St Kilda		260	.	2 6
	1 box					
	1 bdle Hoops S Ferguson "				.	2

Charges paid at

Cartage,

Settled, 190   —FOR JOHN M'CALLUM & CO,   £

TELEGRAPHIC ADDRESS: "M'CALLUM," GLASGOW.
TELEPHONE No. 1462.

10 ANN STREET, (CITY).

Glasgow, 28th Sept. 1900

The MacLeod of MacLeod Dunvegan

For FREIGHT to WEST HIGHLANDS, per Steam-Packet "HEBRIDES."
(FOR CONDITIONS OF CARRIAGE SEE BACK HEREOF.)

MARKS & NOS.	GOODS.			Weight or Measurement		AMOUNT.
June 23	3 trusses tweed 2 pckgs	St Kilda to Obisdale		954		1 . 6
	1 bale 1 chest 1 box					
	1 hpr. 1 portmanteau	to McKenzie St Kilda				
July 7	1 furpoltied	" McKinnon "		958		3 .
	1 pane glass	" McDonald "				
	1 skylight	" Ferguson "				
Aug 18	1 window 1 ck oil	Dvgn to St Kilda		970		5 .

Charges paid at

Cartage,

Settled   —For JOHN M'CALLUM & CO,   £ 1 8 6

For John M'Callum & Co.

Bills of lading, 1903, from John McCallum to John Mackenzie or the MacLeod of MacLeod at Dunvegan, mostly pertaining to goods carried to or from St Kilda.

in respect of their all-year mail contract to Colonsay and Soay (off Skye) and the summer service to St Kilda. By 1895 there were six mails to and from St Kilda by these ships. Even MacLeod's factor John Mackenzie ceased making his independent trips to the island, travelling by the tourist steamers instead.

In 1897 the two steamers made seven trips between them and delivered 208 letters and twenty-five parcels. The number of letters taken off the island was estimated to be about 500, five times the number collected in 1879. St Kilda was therefore satisfactorily serviced in the summer, but still for nine months of the year was condemned to virtual isolation.

However, with the development of steam fishing vessels at this time, a solution was found to the problem. The new steamboats had a greater range than the older sailing vessels and this now put the rich fishing grounds of the north-west within the reach of Aberdeen and Fleetwood fishermen. In the 1890s the steam line-fishers from Aberdeen began fishing for cod and halibut on the banks west of St Kilda and these vessels often called at the island en route to mend their gear or shelter from gales and picked up any mail which the islanders wished to post. Conversely an informal arrangement came about whereby mail for the St Kildans would be addressed to the care of the ship-owners. The sailing time from Aberdeen to St Kilda was thirty-six hours on average. During the winter of 1897-8 the steam fishing boat *Evening Star* made no fewer than twenty-five trips to St Kilda, and delivered mail on each occasion.

A small paragraph in the *Glasgow Herald* of 23 January 1898 announcing the death of Finlay Gillies, a St Kildan youth, and adding that the news had been conveyed by fishing boat, caught the attention of the postal authorities, who quickly seized on the unofficial arrangement at Aberdeen as the standard way of getting mail to St Kilda in wintertime. It was announced in the *Post Office Circular* of 10 May 1898 that 'All correspondence for the island of St Kilda should for the future be sent to Aberdeen'. No question of paying the skippers of these vessels arose, the head postmaster of Aberdeen and the people of St Kilda relying entirely on the goodwill of the fishermen.

By the end of the nineteenth century, therefore, St Kilda, with a population of eighty, enjoyed a reasonable mail service both summer and winter. There was as yet no question of establishing a post office on the island. Money to pay for the postage of outgoing letters was handed over to the skippers and they stamped the letters on arrival in Aberdeen. Mail going from Aberdeen to St Kilda went in sealed mailbags but no-one was officially responsible for them on arrival. It was left to the minister, the Rev. Angus Fiddes, to sort the mail at the manse gate and distribute the letters to their eager recipients.

Aberdeen trawlers in Village Bay, 1902. Due to changes in the type of fish found in the waters around St Kilda, it has attracted trawlers from Aberdeen at certain times and those from Fleetwood at others. Such fluctuations in the fishing affected the routing of mail to the island from time to time.

John Mackenzie, who, it will be remembered, was also the postmaster of Dunvegan, applied to the General Post Office in the autumn of 1899 for the establishment of a sub-post office on St Kilda. It was estimated that mail to St Kilda that year had amounted to 95 letters and 15 parcels sent from Oban and 150 letters and 10 parcels sent via Dunvegan, while approximately 500 pieces of mail had left the island. The Surveyor at Edinburgh reported to the Secretary of the Post Office, London, that there was no real need for either a sub-office or house-to-house delivery since the mail was so small. Sending sealed bags to St Kilda, however, with no-one responsible for receiving them, was without precedent and so it was deemed well to have a sub-postmaster appointed. At first it was proposed only to have the office open for the three summer months at a salary of £2 per annum, but eventually it was agreed to extend its opening all year round for a salary of £5.

Officially the St Kilda post office was established on 20 September 1899 (the date of the GPO minute authorising it) and a single circle date-stamp and type box were despatched from Edinburgh in October. However, it is doubtful whether the office actually began functioning until 2 July 1900, the date on which Fiddes was formally appointed postmaster. A brass mailbag seal was despatched on 25 May 1900, presumably on board either the *Dunara* or the *Hebrides*, and the first recorded date of use of the dates-tamp was in July 1900.

One of the rooms on the ground floor of the factor's house (the bedroom of the officer commanding the military detachment from 1958 to 1966) was converted into a post office where the reverend postmaster dispensed postage stamps and sold postcards to the tourists. Picture postcards were not sanctioned by the Post Office until 1894 and were very slow to catch on thereafter. The earliest series of St Kilda cards, utilising photographs taken by Cherry Kearton in 1896, had a space on the picture side for the sender's message. A later series, with full-size pictures in monochrome, consisted of photographs of St Kilda and groups of islanders taken in 1884 by the Aberdeen photographer, David Whyte, on behalf of George Washington Wilson. Many of his graphic St Kilda studies, the best known of which was the St Kilda Parliament scene, were originally sold to the tourists as full plate sepia photographs mounted on pasteboard.

The Edwardian globetrotter sent postcards by the score and those who reached St Kilda were no exception. A report of a visit to St Kilda, published in the *Oban Times* of 16 June 1901 described how Fiddes boarded the *Dunara Castle* with the island's outgoing mailbag shortly before she weighed anchor: 'The only use I could see for the bag was to bring away the correspondence of the passengers, many of whom had been busy on Saturday and Sunday writing Postcards, etc. from St Kilda and posting them when they got there.' There was no shop on the island nor any organised outlet for the sale of the islanders' produce. Fiddes held a modest stock of stamps consisting of halfpenny and penny values alone, suitable for inland postcards and letters and the foreign postcard rate.

This report reinforces the view that, at that early date, the various sets of postcards by DRM, Russell of Edinburgh, Whyte, Wilson and Valentine were retailed on board the tourist steamers. James Wood, writing in 1903, relates that the postmaster of Lochmaddy (under which St Kilda was placed) reported that an average of 600 postcards were written and posted on each steamer visit, and confirmed that the cards were sold on the steamers. Judging by the messages written on many of them, they were written before reaching the island and their only connection with St Kilda was that they were date-stamped there. It also explains the high proportion of St Kilda postcards written aboard ship but actually posted at the next port of call, which might be anywhere from Callanish on the north-west coast of Lewis to Greenock itself.

Of 2,548 pieces of mail posted at St Kilda in the year August 1907 to August 1908, no fewer than 1,456 were picture postcards. The last mail from the island in August 1906 contained the staggering number of 758 picture postcards alone. It is surprising, in view of the vast number of St Kilda cards posted, that relatively few have survived. The majority of those which have turned up in Edwardian postcard albums bear August dates.

In April 1901 Mr Gibson was sent from Harris to take the decennial census of St Kilda. At this unseasonable time of year neither the *Dunara Castle* nor the *Hebrides* was scheduled to visit the island – not because the weather was too rough for them but because it would have been highly unprofitable at a time when there were no tourists. Due to the lack of transport, and because this was official Government business, it was therefore deemed appropriate to 'send a gunboat'. Gone were the days of *Jackal* and *Flirt*. The ship detailed for this duty was HMS *Bellona*, a steel third-class cruiser, a product of the Naval Defence Programme, built by Messrs Hawthorne, Leslie & Co. of Newcastle-upon-Tyne and launched at their Hepburn yard in 1890. She mounted six guns, and her twin screws developed 4,700hp, giving her a cruising speed of 19 knots. She had a gross tonnage of 1,830 and a length of 280ft, with a 13ft draught. She was commissioned at Devonport in August 1894 and assigned to the Channel Squadron under Commander Paul W. Bush, but at the turn of the century she was based in the Firth of Clyde. She had three masts, two funnels and rakish lines, an impressive sight and by far the largest ship to visit St Kilda up to that time.

Her arrival in Village Bay roused the greatest excitement, especially as it was soon followed by the greatest spectacle the island ever beheld. The ship's boats were launched and headed for the new jetty where presently there came ashore a party of Royal Marines and bluejackets armed with rifles and fixed bayonets. The ship's officers, in frock coats with gold lace epaulettes and bearing swords, formed up and, accompanied by the ship's brass band, presented arms to the strains of the National Anthem after Commander Bush had formally announced the accession of His Majesty King Edward VII.

The *Bellona* was the sixth ship of the Royal Navy to bear the name of the Roman goddess who was wife of Mars, god of war. Five years after her visit to St Kilda she was decommissioned and sold. While Gibson took the census, the ship's surgeon attended to the many and varied ailments of the islanders. The cruiser delivered a consignment of books and magazines, the gift of a well-wisher in Greenock. Of more practical use, however, was a quantity of used naval uniforms, eagerly snapped up by the St Kildans. This explains the nautical rig, complete with brass buttons, sported by many of the islanders in the ensuing years, notably on 26 June 1902 when the entire population was on parade to celebrate the Coronation of King Edward VII and Queen Alexandra. On this occasion the *Hebrides* brought out a large party of Yorkshire tourists (mainly from Bradford) headed by Sir Theophilus Peel, Baronet and High Sheriff of Yorkshire, accompanied by Lady Peel, who presented a Union Jack and distributed white-metal Coronation medals to the entire adult population, the children receiving bronze medals.

The flag was run up a hastily improvised flagpole and the be-medalled St Kildans gave three lusty cheers. Dr Charles Forshaw of Bradford conveyed a personal message from King Edward saying that circumstances prevented him from visiting the island in person but he wished them a good season of fulmar catching. And Queen Alexandra herself got in on the act, sending, via the good doctor, 'large and beautifully executed photographs of their Majesties, each bearing the inscription "a gift to the St Kildans from Her Majesty the Queen with her good wishes"'. As well as their medals, the children received a consignment of picture books from the publisher Sir George Newnes, along with a prodigious amount of other books totalling about half a ton. Angus Fiddes was not present on this auspicious occasion – for reasons which will later become apparent – but doubtless he was later gratified to receive a personal gift from the Rev. F. St John Corbett, rector of Long Marton, Carlisle, consisting of a bound volume of his original sermons. Sir Tristram Tempest of Tong Hall, Yorkshire, contributed two dozen enamelled Coronation mugs for the children, while the Mayor of Bradford had arranged for the royal messages to be printed so that every St Kildan received a copy. The journalist who reported this farrago of nonsense for the *Oban Times* concluded patronisingly that, with such an abundance of wonderful gifts, 'the St Kilda people are likely to be in clover for a considerable time to come'.

On this occasion the *Hebrides* anchored in Village Bay at 2 a.m. of Thursday 26 June. Despite the extremely early hour, the ship gave some sharp blasts of her steam whistle, rudely disturbing the slumbers of the unsuspecting inhabitants. As it happens, the Coronation planned for that very day was delayed because of the King's sudden illness – but no matter, St Kilda celebrated exactly as the Yorkshire tourists had planned 'as the opportunity might not arise again'. At a more civilised hour the sixty-one passengers were ferried ashore and formed up in front of the manse to witness the hoisting of the flag performed by Dr Mitchell of Ballater, while the Fenton sisters from Edinburgh led the singing of the National Anthem. For several years one or other of these ladies had come out to St Kilda each summer to deputise for Fiddes during his annual leave. Dr Forshaw read out an interminable number of messages – according to Alexander Gillies Ferguson who was present on this august occasion and rendered impromptu translations into Gaelic for the benefit of his fellow islanders.

Above: Coronation Day, 1902. The entire population of the island is on parade beside the new flagpole. The islanders are proudly wearing their souvenir medals, while the girls are in their best bib and tucker.

Right: Coronation Medal bearing the conjoined profiles of King Edward VII and Queen Alexandra, given to the author by Alexander Gillies Ferguson (in the photograph he is the tallest figure on the left side of the pole).

Group of St Kildans with the captain of the *Dunara Castle* (Valentine postcard, around 1900). The islanders are seated outside the wall of the manse near the garden gate. Many other versions of this postcard were subsequently produced by Valentine with the skipper removed from the picture and various Highland backgrounds in place of the manse wall. In these cards the group were merely captioned as Highlanders, but they were unmistakeable – especially the poor man with the bandaged face.

St Kilda's practical response to all this largesse was provided by Finlay McQueen, the island's most celebrated cragsman of the period. With appropriate dignity and solemnity he presented a stuffed fulmar and blown eggs for the King and Queen, adding a petition for better medical provision: 'If the authorities should think of appointing a lady medical schoolmistress or missionary it would be a great boon.' The islanders accepted the gifts of tobacco and sweets with their customary grace and then got straight down to the important business of selling their goods. At least one correspondent was somewhat taken aback by 'the strong commercial instinct exhibited by the islanders, who seemed more interested in the sale of their eggs, socks and other wares than in the ceremonies they were asked to witness'.

On 29 May 1901 the *Hebrides* had conveyed to St Kilda the Rev. Archibald Beaton from Muir of Ord to assist Fiddes with the annual communion service. He brought news of the merger which had been effected between the United Presbyterian Church and the Free Church. Robert Rainy was appointed first Moderator of the General Assembly of the United Free Church, as it was thereafter called. Although many Free Church congregations accepted the union, a sizeable number in the Highlands and Islands refused, and thus a greatly diminished Free Church continued. Fiddes was an enthusiast for the union and at first this was accepted by his tiny congregation. However, by August 1901 a dispute between the minister and his flock had developed.

The *Dunara Castle* made her first trip of the season to St Kilda on Sunday 23 June and, although it was the Sabbath, two island boats went out to the steamer shortly after midday. The journal kept by A. Rutherford, one of the passengers, indicates that religious observance was not now as strict as it had formerly been. Rutherford's account was one of the more subjective: 'We expected something wonderful. I do not think we would have been surprised if we had found them dressed like Choctaw Indians in paint and feathers' was a not untypical comment. When the passengers went ashore they were immediately greeted by the islanders at the top of the jetty, where tobacco, sweets and copper coins were eagerly accepted.

The ship had on board the MacLeod of MacLeod who spent much of his time ashore in conference with the minister. It appears that the MacLeod feared that there might be a dispute concerning the ecclesiastical property, technically belonging to the Free Church. At this time the prospect of a fishing station was also very promising and the MacLeod and his factor had come to the conclusion that a new church and manse might have to be erected, possibly somewhere behind the village and near the ancient burial ground. If the Free Church relinquished its buildings they might either be utilised for the fishing station or new premises erected on that site. In the event this proved to be idle speculation. The fishing station never materialised and the church remained where it was.

Early in August 1901 the *Hebrides* called and Fiddes took this opportunity to leave St Kilda for his annual holiday. Several St Kildans accompanied him on this voyage, intent on visiting the Glasgow Exhibition at Kelvingrove. At the end of that month the old *Hebridean* brought the St Kilda tourists back from their jaunt to the big city and it seems probable that Fiddes was also on board. A fortnight later, the *Hebrides* made her last trip of the season and carried the provisions which were intended for the inhabitants of the manse (Fiddes, his housekeeper, and the young schoolmaster, Roderick Campbell) through the coming winter, but the St Kildans refused to offload the minister's stores. Aboard the *Hebrides* was the Rev. Alexander Lee, Mission Superintendent for the Highlands and Islands, who had been despatched in order to settle the dispute. But the St Kildans were not amenable to soothing words or sweet reason, and Lee sailed off into the Hebrides with the minister's stores still in the cargo hold. When the ship reached the Sound of Harris, Lee went ashore at Obbe to try and hire a boat to take the minister's provisions back to St Kilda but failed in this desperate attempt. The inhabitants of the manse would have starved that winter had it not been for the resourcefulness of young Campbell who spent much of his time at the Point of Coll with his fishing line.

An Edwardian picture postcard showing the *Dunara Castle* at Loch Skipport, South Uist, one of her many ports of call in the Outer Hebrides.

There is a general impression that has persisted to this day that the dispute between Fiddes and his congregation was as a result of the unification of the churches. The *Glasgow Weekly Mail* seems to have been responsible for this canard, backed up by some silly correspondence in the *Oban Times*. When the *Hebrides* broke the winter seclusion of St Kilda in late May 1902, Alexander Ferguson was one of the passengers, come to arrange for the wholesaling of the island's produce as a more suitable alternative to the traditional medium of the factor, but also to find out for himself what all the fuss was about. He soon learned that the inhabitants were quite agreeable to becoming adherents of the United Free Church and were at pains to explain that the dispute with Fiddes was quite unconnected with that. A few weeks later, the *Dunara Castle* arrived and on this occasion brought out a delegation from the United Free Church, led by the Rev. Archibald Beaton of Urray near Muir of Ord, Ross-shire, to enquire into the dispute. Whatever the true causes of the dispute, they remained a close secret.

Major Colquhoun of Luss, a St Kilda habitué since 1894 who spent several extended holidays on the island and got to know the islanders quite intimately, wrote an article published in the *Aberdeen Daily Journal* of 17 January 1903 which hinted that the dispute was really all about power: the islanders wanted St Kilda for themselves without any outside supervision, however well-intentioned or benign. The way Colquhoun told it, the campaign against the minister was orchestrated by one or two individuals 'no longer on the island'. On one occasion a party of angry islanders had invaded the manse and virtually assaulted Fiddes. Three attempts were made to land the minister's winter supplies and each time the St Kildans belligerently thwarted them. In the end a relatively small quantity of coal was landed from a Fleetwood trawler so that the manse had a modicum of heat over the winter.

Colquhoun averred that the St Kildans had now got what they wanted: the freedom to do as they pleased. Even the MacLeod of MacLeod had virtually washed his hands of them. It was from this period that various attempts to dispose of the island date, potential purchasers ranging from Christian Salvesen the whaling magnate to John Mackenzie, who rather fancied the notion of switching from factor to laird of St Kilda. But nothing came of these notions and the MacLeod did not actually sell the island until after its inhabitants were evacuated.

The gallant major provided a trenchant comment which, though harsh, was probably not far from the truth: 'What they want, as, to them, the richer "harvest of the sea", is the harvest of the tourist season and of "personally conducted tours" on and around the island by field naturalists and others with long purses and with no "Manse" further to interfere with them. They have shown themselves to be ungrateful, greedy and mercenary. They seem in reality to care as little for the United Free Church of Scotland as now they care for the Church of their ancestors…'

Fiddes boarded the *Dunara Castle* and left St Kilda with the United Free Church delegation. Ostensibly, he was going south on his annual holidays, but he in fact resigned his post at the end of July. He returned to the island on the *Hebrides* in mid-August, but only to pack up his personal belongings. He had one last religious ceremony to perform – conducting a brief service to celebrate His Majesty's Coronation. This was in marked contrast to the pantomime back in June and was mainly conducted in Gaelic. The flag was run up the pole at 'approximately the hour the King was crowned' while Major Colquhoun led the singing of the National Anthem. It was all so much more tasteful and truly in keeping with the spirit of St Kilda.

Fiddes left St Kilda for good aboard the *Hebrides*, accompanied by his cow. He had wished to leave the beast in the care of Catherine MacLennan, who had agreed to remain on the island as manse housekeeper, but the St Kildans were adamant that henceforward no missionary would have grazing rights in what was (and still is) known as the Minister's Glebe or Meadow. It was a final act of petty vindictiveness which showed the islanders in a bad light.

By contrast, the Scottish press generally gave poor Fiddes a sympathetic and affectionate send-off. He continued for some time as a missionary on the mainland, but he never came back to the island where he had laboured so long and to such great advantage to its inhabitants. Ironically, he was serving as a missionary on Unst, most northerly of the Shetland Isles, when a message from the sea was washed up there and found to contain an urgent plea from St Kilda, dated 20 October 1902, for a few tons of coal to see them through the long, hard winter. Fiddes retired to Portmahomack where he died a few years later, allegedly a bitter and disillusioned man who never recovered from the unkindness and ingratitude with which he had latterly been treated.

In June 1902 the United Free Church delegation had brought with them young Lachlan MacLean from Tiree who was left behind as a temporary substitute for Fiddes, but who was formally appointed 'teacher-missionary' on 8 September and served the religious needs of the islanders for twelve months. In turn he was succeeded by John Fraser on 19 October 1903. Angus Fiddes was the last ordained minister to serve on St Kilda, although two of the missionaries who followed in his footsteps were subsequently ordained.

Seven

Enter the Trawlers

By 1903 Alexander Gillies Ferguson was established at 93 Hope Street on his own account. His ambition had been to supplant the factors who had traditionally been accused of buying St Kilda produce at the lowest rates and charging top price for imported goods. Eventually he achieved his first goal and visited the island each summer in his yacht *Colonsay*. He gave his friends and relatives a fair deal and they trusted him implicitly, but by 1903 he had also taken over the factor's role in providing St Kilda with the luxury items it required. That this procedure was carried out not only with the knowledge of the factor but also at his behest is borne out by the documents preserved at Dunvegan Castle. There is a letter from Ferguson to John Mackenzie on notepaper with the printed heading: 'A.G. Ferguson, Glasgow and at St Kilda Island, N.B.', dated 1 September 1903. With the letter was a detailed list of the goods supplied to each of the eighteen families, totalling £26 19s 7½d 'to your esteemed orders in June'. More significantly, however, the letter refers to Ferguson undertaking 'to dispose of your entire stock of St Kilda Tweed and at the best possible prices… Please forward the Tweed according to my last letter as soon as possible stating terms'. Ferguson also mentioned the fact that the *Hebrides* had failed to effect a landing in August due to bad weather but that 'I believe she will make another attempt on 7th inst'.

In the same year John McCallum and Co. moved from Ann Street to more commodious premises at 36 Oswald Street in the heart of Glasgow, a stone's throw from the Broomielaw. At that time it was said that the throng of ships large and small was so tightly packed that it was possible to cross the Clyde by jumping from one deck to another. From this year dates a bill to John Mackenzie for freight sent to St Kilda and consigned by the *Hebrides* on 25 July, 14 August and 29 August. The consignment on 25 July included a box of Glasgow bread; St Kilda, like other parts of the Western Isles, had acquired a taste for Glasgow stale bread and given up home-baking. This was one of the less acceptable aspects of the increased frequency of steamer visits.

Another was the relatively easy access which the steamers provided for English dealers in rare birds' eggs. In 1906 and 1907 Harry Brazenor of Manchester made trips to St Kilda, arriving on the *Dunara Castle* at the end of May and departing on the *Hebrides* in September in both years, gathering the eggs of two dozen species, including the St Kilda wren and Leach's fork-tailed petrel. He arrived in the nesting season and, as well as taking the eggs, he later collected both immature and adult birds for their skins. He went so far as to prepare a leaflet which he mailed to prospective clients, promising to provide for the sum of £15 a 'large and comprehensive collection'. The specimens would be delivered 'in the form of first-class cabinet skins'. Apart from the educational value of such a series of British birds, 'many are likely to greatly increase in value owing to their growing scarcity and to the increasing stringency of the Wild Bird protection laws'. The St Kilda wren, in fact, had the distinction of its very own Act of Parliament (15 August 1904), but this did not deter Brazenor and others like him. The St Kildans themselves regarded the birdlife as fair game, and had moved quite a long way since Skirving's visit, appreciating that there was more one could do with a dead fulmar than eat it.

Lachlan MacLean relinquished his duties, spiritual, educational and postal, to John Fraser on 19 October 1903. Many years later F.G. Rea published an account of his time as a schoolmaster in South Uist (1890–1913) and describes a visit to Lochboisdale on the *Dunara Castle*, which had on board a young 'missionary, schoolmaster, registrar and postmaster' of St Kilda whose sojourn on the island had driven him 'quite insane'. Michael Robson (2005) conjectured that Lachlan MacLean was the unfortunate young man, but Rea added that the missionary could not speak Gaelic and was therefore very isolated, whereas MacLean, a native of Tiree, was a fluent Gaelic speaker. Fraser, on the other hand, hailed from Inverness and seems to fit the description. He probably left St Kilda at the end of May 1906, when the *Dunara* paid her first visit that year. In turn, he was succeeded by Peter MacLachlan, who was formally appointed on 16 August 1906. He was a much older man, in his fortieth year and the first married man to minister to the St Kildans since the departure of Neil Mackenzie in 1844; his young wife Alice gave birth to a daughter, Flora, in 1909. In view of the mental condition of his young predecessor – probably a breakdown such as one of the Army doctors suffered half a century later – it must have seemed prudent to appoint a man of more mature years, with the stability of a good marriage as an antidote to the loneliness of such a remote situation.

The missionary-teachers who continued until the evacuation in 1930 could not perform the sacraments of baptism, marriage or communion and these functions were carried out by ordained ministers who visited St Kilda each July. Sometimes they arrived by one steamer and left by another a week or ten days later. Conversely, in some periods, the functions of teacher and missionary were separate, and various young men and women conducted the school. The women generally came for a month or two to teach sewing and other domestic skills. A more frequent service by the *Dunara Castle* and *Hebrides*, mainly driven by the burgeoning tourist industry, ensured greater flexibility in the coming and going of missionaries, teachers and ministers from 1905 onwards. During the three years of the MacLachlan mission, his wife Alice conducted the school.

Though remaining as missionary on the island till the autumn of 1909, MacLachlan resigned his postmastership on 15 December 1906 in favour of Neil Ferguson, the ground officer who held the post until the evacuation. During MacLachlan's brief postmastership he wrote to John Weir, MP for the Western Isles, suggesting that the Northern Lighthouse Commissioners' steamer *Hesperus*, which visited the Monach and Flannan lighthouses (both about 40 miles from St Kilda) monthly, be diverted to St Kilda with mail and provisions, but the Lighthouse Commissioners of the early twentieth century were no more helpful than their predecessors.

Nevertheless, MacLachlan's letter struck an optimistic note: 'Severe as the weather has occasionally been, there has not been a day on which boats could not land. There is a nice little pier here, most convenient for small boats landing.' He mentioned that the steam trawler *Diadem* had been coming to St Kilda that winter and asked Mr Weir to address his reply via Fleetwood in Lancashire.

The General Post Office had sounded the Northern Lighthouse Commissioners three years earlier, but they had refused to co-operate. The postal authorities tried again in 1906 and got no reply. They persisted in March 1907 and eventually extracted a reply from the commissioners stating blandly that there had been no change in circumstances since their last letter of 1903.

In that year Donald Craig, skipper of the Aberdeen trawler *Brilliant Star*, paid his first visit to St Kilda. The first steam trawlers to reach St Kilda had been documented in the diary of John Ross in 1889, who noted that: 'The landing of

Dunara Castle in Village Bay. In the background is the island of Dùn, St Kilda's bulwark against southerly storms in which the sea has been known to come right over the topmost ridge. In the foreground are some of the drystone structures known as cleits. The church, manse and schoolhouse are on the extreme left.

men off any of these strange vessels is the cause of the greatest consternation in the island, even in these enlightened times.' The first trawler apparently anchored in Glen Bay and its crew then clambered up the cliffs and advanced up the Great Glen, to the alarm of the women who were tending their sheep near the Amazon's House and immediately rushed home with cries of *Tha Goill air a Ghleann* ('foreigners are in the Glen').

Many years later, Tom Steel interviewed Craig and obtained an invaluable reminiscence. 'When I went ashore,' he said, 'I fell in love with the St Kildan people and they fell for me.' He was proud of the fact that he introduced the boys of St Kilda to football and provided Steel with a vivid account of a football match in which the missionary's family played against an island team composed of four boys and four girls. Craig allegedly introduced the first looking-glass to the island, a pocket mirror which he gave to Norman MacQueen. When Norman's wife found the mirror under his pillow she thought it was a picture of a woman he was looking at, but when she looked at it she snorted, 'Huh, she's not a beauty anyway!'

Craig also founded the White Man's League of Friendship, the office-bearers consisting of God as President, Jesus as Vice President and 'Donald McBain Craig, DSC, RD, the Recruiting Officer'. On one of his visits to St Kilda he presented each inhabitant with a small wooden dagger which they were supposed to wear round their necks. There was a swearing-in ceremony, at which the islanders solemnly held up their daggers and recited: 'By the help of God, may the day that I betray my fellow man or woman, may this dagger pierce my heart. Fear God, fear no man.'

There was a close bond between the St Kildans and the trawlermen. Both communities were accustomed to hardship and danger. Loss of life at sea brought the fishermen close to their God and they were almost universally very devout, often belonging to fundamentalist sects such as the Jehovah's Witnesses and the Exclusive Brethren. Close ties between the St Kildans and the crews extended over several generations, and several of the trawler owners named their boats and their homes after St Kilda. In time, the St Kildans would come to rely on the trawlers for regular communication in the winter months. The numbers of trawlers not only fluctuated according to the state of the fishing, but also depended largely on the type of fish trawled, which explains why Aberdeen or Fleetwood, but seldom both simultaneously, were St Kilda's conduits to the outside world.

The Fleetwood steam trawler *Kilda*, from a picture postcard of 1924. St Kilda had close ties with the Lancashire fishing port which endured from Victorian times until the advent of the military garrison in the late 1950s when the winter address was PO Box 99 Fleetwood, whence the mail was directed.

In the Edwardian era the Post Office re-examined the arrangement for getting mail to and from St Kilda by trawler. They discovered that Captain Ritchie, skipper of the *Evening Star* of Aberdeen, who had taken mail on numerous occasions in 1905, no longer intended fishing the St Kilda banks. Cod and halibut had deserted these fishing grounds in favour of dogfish, which was not acceptable in the Aberdeen fish market. Dogfish and other 'rough stuff', however, were suitable to the English fried fish and chips industry and, from 1906 onwards, Fleetwood trawlers began fishing in the area. The St Kildans were not slow in switching their mailing system, hence the arrangement with the *Diadem*.

For some time an informal arrangement had existed between the postmaster of Aberdeen and the trawler skippers by which a small *ex gratia* payment of 10s was made every time mail was brought in from or taken out to St Kilda. With the change to despatch via Fleetwood the Post Office approached Messrs Kelly, owners of two Fleetwood trawlers, but they demanded £10 a return trip and undertook on those terms to make five trips to St Kilda between November and June. The Post Office, however, maintained their principle that although the trawlers took the mail they were not bound to land it if it was inconvenient. The 10s payment was merely a form of acknowledgement for this and not meant as payment in fulfilment of a contract. When this was put to them, Messrs Kelly magnanimously agreed to take the mail on their trawlers for nothing. Nevertheless the practice of giving 10s to the skippers was continued by the head postmaster of Fleetwood.

The change in the routing of St Kilda mail was authorised in the *Post Office Circular* of 30 October 1906 which stated: 'All correspondence for St Kilda should be sent to Fleetwood until further instructions are issued in the *Post Office Circular*.'

In the winter of 1906–7 Albert Walkner, in command of the Fraserburgh trawler *Knowsie*, earned a reputation in the trawling fraternity for returning to port with record catches. No one could work out where he fished, but the suspicion grew that he must be fishing within the 3-mile limit imposed by the Fishery Board. On Sunday 14 April 1907 the fishery cruiser *Minna*, apparently acting on a tip-off, caught the *Knowsie* with her trawl down, a couple of miles north of Boreray. Walkner later claimed that he was not breaking the law as he was actually 5 miles from Hirta, but the Fishery Board claimed that the sea within a 3-mile radius of Boreray was also within the proscribed limits. Walkner thought the ship was a Norwegian whaler and did not realise that she was a fishery cruiser until she was within hailing distance. The captain of the *Minna* put a man on board the *Knowsie* and ordered Walkner to follow him to Village Bay.

By the time the *Minna* and the *Knowsie* anchored, the entire population of St Kilda had congregated on the jetty, with Peter MacLachlan, their minister, in the forefront. It was later alleged in Lochmaddy Sheriff Court that the missionary had harangued the crew of the fishery cruiser in Gaelic and English. At any rate, the St Kildans became 'very excited and threatening'. When tempers cooled, the *Minna's* skipper learned that Walkner was a great favourite with the islanders. He had agreed to transport the wife of William Macdonald from St Kilda to a hospital in Aberdeen where she needed urgent treatment. MacLachlan told the *Minna's* crew that her blood would be on their heads if they arrested the trawler skipper. MacLachlan finally made the impassioned plea: the *Minna* could arrest every other trawler in the area, but please, not this one. The *Knowsie* not only fished round St Kilda with the permission of the islanders, but also with their blessing!

The *Minna's* captain remained obdurate and insisted that the trawler proceed to North Uist to be dealt with at the Sheriff Court in Lochmaddy. Thereupon MacLachlan, accompanied by five islanders (Neil Ferguson, Ewan Gillies, Donald McQueen and Mr and Mrs William Macdonald), insisted on travelling in the *Knowsie* in order to give evidence in support of Captain Walkner. Despite their pleas in mitigation, the St Kildans were powerless to prevent the law taking its course. Walkner was found guilty and fined £90 or thirty days in jail. Being unable or unwilling to pay the fine he was taken into custody and sent on to Inverness Prison. The *Knowsie*, under command of the mate, left Lochmaddy and sailed round the north of Scotland back to Aberdeen – with the St Kilda delegation still aboard. When they got there the St Kildans hired Messrs Wilson and Duffus (Advocates) to draft a petition to the Scottish Office on Walkner's behalf, to have his sentence remitted or reduced.

The St Kildans were not only put to considerable expense but were also stranded in Aberdeen for several weeks awaiting the outcome of their appeal. Although it was unsuccessful, the saga of the *Knowsie* gained the island some useful publicity. Walkner was portrayed as a saint who had helped the St Kildans on countless occasions, and this was sharply contrasted with the pusillanimity of Messrs Dewar and Weir, successive MPs for the Western Isles, who had signally failed to do anything to help their remotest constituents. Putting this affair in context it should be noted that on the same day that Walkner was convicted at Lochmaddy the skippers of fourteen Grimsby trawlers, caught fishing illegally in the Moray Firth, were each fined £150 at Elgin Sheriff Court.

Although trawlers from either Aberdeen or Fleetwood continued to carry St Kilda mail right up until the evacuation in 1930, this arrangement operated sporadically, being marked periodically by sordid haggling on the part of the trawler owners. Within two years the system had broken down and Neil Ferguson wrote to J. Hegarty, the head postmaster of Aberdeen, suggesting that the trawlers be subsidised for carrying the mail. Hegarty reported to the Secretary of the Post Office, Edinburgh, on 23 June 1908, recommending that the ship letter rate (a farthing per piece) be levied on the St Kilda mail and paid to the trawlermen. As this would have raised only a few pence he also suggested hopefully: 'Possibly a letter conveying some words of the Postmaster General's appreciation would meet the case.'

Hegarty approached the Aberdeen trawling company of Bookless Bros, whose trawlers had made eleven despatches to St Kilda in the winters of 1907 and 1908. In the absence of Mr Bookless, a junior official said that no payment was wanted and that it was a pleasure to be of service. A fortnight later, however, Bookless himself wrote to Hegarty saying that payment was wanted, and regretting the contradictory impression conveyed by his subordinate. Bookless demanded £10 a trip, but the Post Office offered 10s. Bookless considered this sum ridiculous but cut his figure to £2. The Post Office then compromised by offering £1 for collection and delivery, or 10s for one way only. It should be borne in mind that the revenue based on the actual postage on the mail carried never amounted to more than 4s in winter.

Bookless agreed to the Post Office terms and now coolly demanded payment at these rates for past services, adding: 'Shall be glad if you will have a statement made out of mails already carried and favour us with remittance at your earliest convenience.' No exact records had been kept, though by this time (October 1908) Bookless trawlers had made fourteen despatches to, and eleven collections of mail from, St Kilda. The Post Office then offered £5 for these past services and this was accepted without a murmur. From February 1909 onwards returns of the number of mail-trips were kept and furnished for accounting purposes every three months.

This arrangement, which looked like being the final solution to the problem of St Kilda's winter mails, came to an abrupt end within a matter of months. The Bookless trawler *Bannerdale* made no fewer than ten trips to St Kilda between 21 October 1908 and 26 March 1909. The reason for this surprising frequency became apparent on the latter date. The Liberal Government had recently introduced old age pensions and an official went to St Kilda in March to find out who was eligible for 5s a week. He was transported by the fishery protection cruiser *Minna*. Not only did they find three septuagenarians eligible for the pension, but also the *Bannerdale* with her trawl down inside the prohibited area. Her skipper turned out to be none other than Albert Walkner, who was duly summoned to appear before the sheriff at Lochmaddy.

Pending the hearing of this case, Bookless Bros wrote to the Secretary of the Post Office in Edinburgh requesting that, in view of Walkner's services rendered to St Kilda by taking mail and provisions, the Secretary of State for Scotland should be approached with a view to mitigating the penalty which they thought would be a £100 fine or six months imprisonment. The Secretary of the Post Office considered that the frequency of trips made by the *Bannerdale* was accounted for by the excellence of the fishing in the prohibited area and therefore replied that the Postmaster General was unable to intervene.

On this occasion Walkner was subsequently fined £50 or thirty days at Lochmaddy Sheriff Court. A somewhat flippant memorandum attached to the file in Post Office Archives comments jocularly: 'Alas for the St Kilda mails; but perhaps the rarer advent of Mails will be compensated for by Old Age Pensions; £50 is a stiff fine. Perhaps Walkner may find it convenient to recoup himself by giving St Kilda a more frequent mail service, or do you think he'll prefer 30 days of "rest and economy" like a suffragette?'

Eighteen months later, however, Bookless Bros apparently relented and even managed to take mail to St Kilda once a fortnight on average. When the rival Don Fishing Co. joined in, St Kilda had four mails in January 1911 alone. The General Post Office in Edinburgh, suspecting illegal trawling and feeling that the trawlermen were overdoing their postal deliveries, urged the head postmaster of Aberdeen not to send mail more often than once a fortnight. Hegarty replied, however, that this might offend the skippers on whose goodwill he depended so much, so finally the matter was left to his discretion. There was an average of forty-eight letters to, and fifty from, St Kilda in these trips, for which the Post Office paid out £1 a round trip.

The island continued to be regularly served by the coastal steamers during the brief summer season. On 13 May 1909 Alexander Ferguson boarded the *Dunara Castle* at the Broomielaw and journeyed to St Kilda on a mercy mission. On 22 March that year an island boat had capsized while attempting to land a party of fowlers on Dùn. Neil MacKinnon and John Gillies were rescued but the others were drowned. One was Donald MacDonald, aged fifty, who left a widow and six children, while the others were Norman McQueen, twenty-three, and his brother John, seventeen. News of this calamity had reached Ferguson by trawler and he immediately launched an appeal in the *Glasgow Herald*, raising about £30 for the relief of the widow and orphans.

The cost of delivering mail to St Kilda was increased when a rural post and delivery was established on 14 November 1910. Ferriage (i.e. for taking mail from the trawler to the jetty and vice versa) was now paid to Neil Ferguson at 1s a time, and 6d was paid for delivering inward letters. This additional emolument was gradually increased until it reached its maximum in 1926 of 3s 6d each way for ferriage and 11d for house-to-house delivery. In 1910 Neil Ferguson's salary was £10 per annum plus a bonus of £2 15s.

On 24 July 1910 the *Hebrides* paid the most important visit of the year (at least in the eyes of the St Kildans), for it brought out the usual delegation of churchmen for the celebration of the annual Communion. Peter MacLachlan, not being ordained, could not conduct this sacrament and thus it fell that year to the Rev. Roderick MacKinnon from Aberfeldy who also took the opportunity to marry Norman MacKinnon and Ann Gillies. In time, they would produce eight children who survived infancy and formed the largest family on the island, but it was their decision to leave in 1930 which made evacuation of the entire population inevitable.

On 19 August the same year, J.A. Smith, 'Contractor to Office of Works', based in Aberdeen, visited St Kilda aboard the *Hebrides* and took a number of excellent photographs, including Village Bay with the *Hebrides* at anchor and a general view of the village, but also two which concentrated on the factor's house in its role of post office, complete with a signboard above the porch door, and a crowd of passengers off the ship clamouring in the doorway to post their cards. In his notes he commented that a record mail was despatched and that the postmaster had to get help to stamp and bag the mail. He also noted that the girl in a white blouse on the right of one photograph was Annie MacLean, the schoolmistress. The window of the room accommodating the post office was festooned with postcards showing the range of views then on sale. Smith subsequently wrote an article entitled 'An Isolated and Intermittent Post Office' for *St Martin's le Grand* (the Post Office magazine). McCallum's flagship had no fewer than seventy-six passengers on board – one more than the total population of St Kilda by that time. Smith mentions that the passengers purchased postcards by the dozen from the ship's steward: 'Their number was increased by letters, written on board at our leisure and kept to be posted on the island, to receive the coveted St Kilda postmark.'

He described the interior of the post office as 'a bare room, the only fittings being a table, desk and window-sill'. Neil Ferguson 'was kept busy retailing postcards at twopence each and selling stamps at their usual face value [a halfpenny]'. He added: 'When at last he locked up the office, carried his mail to the little pier, and thence by boat to the steamer in the bay, we had the satisfaction of learning that the mail was a record one for St Kilda.' Assuming that every passenger despatched just ten postcards, it would, indeed, have been a record.

In another account he mentioned the visit of two policemen who stayed on the island for two weeks between steamers to superintend the dipping of the sheep under recently introduced legislation. A report by the police sergeant from Lochmaddy indicates what a farce this turned out to be, as the large pack of island dogs was quite useless in rounding up the sheep and the men were just as useless when it came to dipping the animals. In the end, the policemen were compelled to do the work themselves, otherwise they would have been stuck on St Kilda indefinitely.

After having four mails in January 1911, St Kilda was, by contrast, cut off by severe gales for three months, ultimately being relieved by HMS *Pathfinder*, a fishery cruiser, which was despatched from Greenock on 15 April 1911 with provisions and mail consisting of 245 letters and thirteen parcels on board. Had it not been for the fact that the ship was engaged on important Government business – the decennial census – she would never have left her base at Auchenlochan in the Kyles of Bute. When she reached St Kilda on Monday 17 April a severe south-easterly gale was blowing so it was impossible to anchor in Village Bay, let alone attempt a landing. The ship headed east to take shelter in West Loch Tarbert, Harris, and returned to St Kilda on the Wednesday morning to find that the storm had only slightly abated. Nevertheless, a boat was lowered and approached the jetty. Landing, however, was impossible. The *Pathfinder* remained uneasily at anchor until that evening, and in the end it was the foolhardy St Kildans themselves who launched a boat and came out to the ship in the desperate hope of picking up the mails she was carrying. The cruiser then weighed anchor as the weather worsened again and put out to sea. Several days later, when the wind eventually veered round to the west, the *Pathfinder* finally managed to put one very sea-sick census-taker on to dry land. It was duly recorded that the population now stood at eighty souls, forty of each sex. There had been three marriages and sixteen live births since the 1901 census, balanced by thirteen deaths in the same period.

On 22 June 1911 the *Dunara Castle* paid a special visit to the island, on the very day that King George V was crowned in Westminster Abbey. This was, in fact, a repetition of the exercise of nine years earlier, although with rather more decorum and taste than the Yorkshire stunt. The large party consisted of about forty gentlemen and twenty ladies, with a good sprinkling of ministers, and was headed by the Lord Lieutenant for Inverness-shire. The passengers and St Kildans mingled together on the level ground above the jetty, between the store house and the manse garden, to hear His Majesty's representative for the county to which St Kilda nominally belonged read out the proclamation, after which the assembled multitude gave three hearty cheers. In fact, the photograph taken of this throng seems to show mainly the visitors, and the only St Kildans appear to be the wee ladies on the extreme left and right foreground. By contrast with 1902, there was no Union Jack and no distribution of Coronation medals or mugs, although the St Kildans wove a special piece of tweed (to which each family contributed part) as a present for King George.

In the same year John McCallum produced the first edition of a handsome, fully illustrated sixteen-page brochure entitled 'Circular Tours', with a picture of the *Hebrides* on the cover. It devoted four pages to the various ports of call from Greenock to Lochmaddy and then seven pages exclusively to St Kilda, giving a true indication of the importance of the latter from the tourism viewpoint. By this time the *Hebrides* was making four or five cruises to St Kilda in June, July and August, but the revenue from the tourist trade, at £10 a head for the round trip including full board, exceeded all normal business. That was a basic price, but there were extra charges for berths in four-berth, two-berth and deck cabins on an ascending scale. The trip usually lasted seven days, but if it were prolonged beyond that time due to bad weather tourists were charged an extra 9s a day for their food. This edition of the brochure claimed that the ship was a 'Splendidly Fitted Steamer, Lighted by Electricity' and that it boasted 'Superior Accommodation, Bathroom, etc'. The reality was rather different, especially for the tourists who did not pay extra for the smaller cabins but opted to sleep in the crowded saloon, which one disillusioned passenger likened to the meanest of doss-houses.

The brochure published by the rival company of Martin Orme for the 'circular tours' of the *Dunara Castle* that year ran to twenty-four pages, but devoted only one page to St Kilda. However, it offered a similar service at exactly the same rates. Perhaps economic measures dictated the down-sizing of Martin Orme's brochure the following year. Although still printed by Peter Bertram of Argyle Street, Glasgow, it now consisted of a single sheet folded to form eight pages, the only illustration being on the cover, depicting the steamer. The description of St Kilda was now reduced to half a page, but this brochure also now intimated that 'The Steamer has Wireless Equipment and carries an Operator. Radio Telegrams can be sent to the Steamer (via MALIN HEAD) from any Post Office, and vice versa'. This was the year in which the *Titanic* was the first ship to send out distress signals by radiotelegraphy and only two years since the *Montcalm* had used wireless to apprehend a murderer, Dr Harvey Hawley Crippen. The *Dunara Castle* might have been quite an old lady by 1912 but she was at the cutting edge of maritime technology. For many years her radio officer was Peter M. Ferguson, himself one of the St Kilda Fergusons.

Proclamation of King George V, June 1911, outside the manse wall, with the store house in the background. By contrast with the picture of the Coronation ceremony in 1902, the St Kildans are virtually absent from this photograph. Indeed, the token islander seems to be the small boy on the extreme right! Most of the onlookers are, in fact, passengers off the steamer, the ladies dressed in the height of fashion with motoring veils securing their wide-brimmed hats against the summer breezes of St Kilda.

Prolonged bad weather over the winter of 1911–12 meant that St Kilda was without mail for four months the following spring. Once more the Aberdeen trawlers had abandoned the St Kilda fishing grounds in favour of the North Sea and no alternative arrangement had been made with the Fleetwood boats. A trawler did call at the island by chance on 15 April and later reported that the St Kildans were worried at the lack of mail, the last letters having been received on 11 December the previous year. By 17 April 329 letters and eighty-three parcels for St Kilda had accumulated at Aberdeen, but no trawler was willing to take the mail. This amount had swollen to 393 letters and ninety-two parcels by 27 May when the *Hebrides* made her first voyage of the season.

GLASGOW AND THE WEST HIGHLANDS

CIRCULAR TOURS

(About Seven Sailing Days)

TO THE OUTER ISLANDS BY THE "HEBRIDES"

Splendidly Fitted Steamer
Lighted by Electricity

Superior Accommodation
Bathroom, etc.

EVERY TEN DAYS

From GLASGOW
at 11 a.m.

and

GREENOCK
at 4.30 p.m.

Leaving Greenock on arrival of Train from (Central Station) Glasgow

*Cabin for the Round, Board included, - £9

Cruises to St. Kilda, Loch Roag, and Loch Scavaig
on Special Dates

*Cabin for Round, Board included, - - £10

FOR DATES OF SAILINGS and BERTHS APPLY TO

JOHN McCALLUM & CO.
87 UNION STREET, GLASGOW, C. 1

Partners { Hugh C. Young
{ Wm. Young

Telegrams : " M'Callum, Glasgow "
Phone : 2193 Central

*Berths in Four-Berthed Rooms, 2/6 extra, in Two-Berthed Rooms and Deck Cabins, 5/- extra; and Passengers remitting by own cheque (London excepted), will please include cost of exchange. Full fare payable at time of booking.

The Tour occupies about Seven Days, but any meals supplied beyond Eight Days for Tourists will be charged at the rate of 9/- per day

A tourist brochure, published by John McCallum for the season of 1912, featuring the *Hebrides*. The florid text of this booklet captures the romantic view of St Kilda which conformed to the public image of the island at the time.

GLASGOW AND THE HIGHLANDS.

CIRCULAR TOURS
(ABOUT SEVEN DAYS)
TO
THE WESTERN ISLES
OF SCOTLAND

By the favourite Steamer

"DUNARA CASTLE,"

From *GLASGOW* (Berth 44, North Side), *every* TEN DAYS, at 11.30 a.m.
and from *GREENOCK* (West Quay), at 4.30 p.m.

*FARE FOR THE ROUND (INCLUDING MEALS), £9

ST. KILDA.

EXTENDED TOURS to this lonely Island on Special Dates
*Fare (Including Meals), £10.

*Berths in Four-Berthed Rooms, 2/6 extra; in Two-Berthed Rooms and Deck Cabin, 5/- extra.

FOR DATES OF SAILINGS AND FOR BERTHS APPLY TO
MARTIN ORME & CO., 20 Robertson Street, GLASGOW, C.2.
TELEGRAPHIC ADDRESS—'ISLESMAN, GLASGOW."
TELEPHONE—CENTRAL, 2453.

Dunara brochure, 1912. Published by the rival company of Martin Orme, it was remarkably similar in style and content to that produced by John McCallum.

In the meantime Captain James Rennie of the trawler *Strathmore* had arrived in Aberdeen on 18 May with the story that the St Kildans were starving. Severe Atlantic gales in the previous four months had kept the trawlers away. A ship bringing provisions had been sent to St Kilda twice without succeeding in landing them due to the weather. When the news of the 'famine' broke, reaction was immediate in an unexpected quarter. The *Daily Mirror* organised a relief expedition, though it was a Saturday and the new Shop Hours Act made it difficult to procure the necessary provisions. Both Sir Thomas Lipton and Sir Joseph Lyons gave generous assistance. Within three hours the *Daily Mirror's* expedition set off from London for Glasgow, where a specially chartered tug, the *Victor*, was standing by. The steel screw tug of 175 tons and 99hp, owned by Steel & Bennie of Glasgow, had a speed of 14 knots and was therefore one of the fastest ships on the Clyde. She left Gourock on Sunday 19 May and arrived at St Kilda in rough seas the following day.

Meanwhile Winston Churchill, then First Lord of the Admiralty, had despatched HMS *Achilles* from Lamlash in the Firth of Clyde to St Kilda with an emergency supply of food. This armoured cruiser was built by Armstrong, Elswick in 1904–7 at a cost of £1,180,000 and had a displacement of 13,350 tons. She bristled with the latest armament, including the great turrets that housed her six 9.2in guns and a brace of 7.5in guns. This mighty Warrior Class cruiser had a top speed of 29 knots and carried a crew of 712 – almost ten times the population of St Kilda. At the beginning of the First World War she was attached to the Mediterranean Squadron and was involved in the hunt for the German battleships *Goeben* and *Breslau*. Later she was based at Freetown, Sierra Leone, but was then transferred back to the 2nd Cruiser Squadron of the Grand Fleet and was sunk on 1 June 1916 at the Battle of Jutland.

Churchill's orders reached the ship on a Saturday morning as the crew were preparing for captain's rounds, but within the hour she had steam up and raced down the Firth at full speed, reaching St Kilda just after 6 a.m. the following morning. After the prolonged storms, Village Bay was like a mill-pond when the mighty cruiser glided to a halt and anchored. The boats were lowered and loaded with provisions, including a generous consignment of tobacco. A veritable flotilla of tenders and cutters headed for the shore, led by a cutter in which Midshipman Angus (later Admiral Sir Angus) Cunninghame-Graham gazed apprehensively at the silent shore. Alongside him was a naval rating armed with a rifle in case the mob, maddened by their lack of food, tried to rush the boats.

When the cutter reached the jetty, however, no one was to be seen, but from the church issued forth the drawn-out sounds of Gaelic psalms. The entire population was at its devotions. When the church emptied the young midshipman was amazed at the apparent indifference of the islanders. Even when Cunninghame-Graham explained the purpose of the visit the St Kildans refused to unload the boats because it was the Sabbath. In the end, the sailors had to unload the boats themselves and discreetly covered the mounds of crates with tarpaulins lest the sight of them give offence to the islanders. The only concession to their appetites was the hamper of newly baked and lusciously buttered bread which the captain sent ashore later in the day. The ravenous St Kildans eagerly devoured the bread, but still refused to move the stores until the Sabbath was out.

By contrast, they worked with great enthusiasm all night to move the supplies into the store house and on Monday afternoon they were invited aboard to inspect the gigantic guns and the engine-room. While the sailors entertained their visitors with jigs and hornpipes the stewards plied the children with lemonade and biscuits. At dawn on Tuesday the cruiser got under way and returned to Lamlash with the satisfaction of having accomplished a great humanitarian mission. Later on, however, there was a great feeling of chagrin and anger at the *Daily Mirror*, which gave lavish coverage to its own mercy mission (which reached St Kilda a day after *Achilles*) but hardly mentioned the Navy's efforts at all.

The *Daily Mirror* telegraphed Captain the Honourable Stanhope Hawke, in command of *Achilles*, and asked him to tell the islanders that help was on the way. When she anchored in Village Bay, Neil Ferguson went aboard and had a message telegraphed to his brother Alexander in Glasgow confirming the report that supplies were short. This was the first telegraphic communication ever made between a resident on St Kilda and the mainland.

For several days the *Daily Mirror* gave the relief of St Kilda prominence, with large headlines and whole pages of photographs. The tug had on board Dr Charles Taylor of Glasgow who spent some time examining the islanders and treating a wide range of minor ailments, the worst being a severe attack of toothache. The newspaper's photographer took numerous pictures of the islanders. Most of the women had their heads covered with shawls which would not be out of place in a fundamentalist Islamic society of the present day, but the image of a toddler in his ill-fitting home-made clothes tugged the nation's heartstrings. The condition of this wee fellow seemed to the world at large to symbolise the backwardness and grinding poverty of the remote island. One reader was moved to do something more permanent for the St Kildans. H. Gordon Selfridge, proprietor of the famous department store in Oxford Street, London, responded to the *Mirror*'s recommendation that a wireless station be erected on the island by immediately donating £100 to the fund. The *Daily Mirror* announced that arrangements for the purchase of wireless telegraphy plant were in hand and that it was hoped that the installation would be completed within the next few weeks. Permission to erect the station was readily given by the MacLeod of MacLeod and an application to the Postmaster General for a licence had been made.

Major Anstruther-Gray MP, raised the question of wireless communication for St Kilda in the House of Commons on 22 May 1912. Six years earlier, John Weir MP had also investigated the possibility of telephone or wireless communication with the island. The PMG replied on that occasion that it would cost £10,000 to lay a cable to St Kilda, or £1,400 to install a wireless telegraph. Since the number of telegrams sent would have been very small, the establishment and maintenance of such a station would have been prohibitive, so Weir's application had not been sanctioned.

In June 1912 John H. Webb, acting on behalf of the *Daily Mirror*, applied for the licence 'in case of urgent need'. It was proposed at first to communicate via the Flannan Lighthouse which had wireless, but the intractable Northern Lighthouse Commissioners flatly refused. Webb then asked for a licence to communicate via Lochboisdale in South Uist and the Scottish Office had no objection. Although suspicious that once communication was established the Post Office would be pressed to take over the installation if the *Daily Mirror* should decide to discontinue its maintenance, the Post Office granted the licence in January 1913. Telegrams were to be sent at ordinary inland rates, but the Post Office reserved the right to raise the charges. The *Daily Mirror* had been too optimistic in thinking that the wireless station would be installed by July 1912 – almost a year passed before the construction was completed.

Meanwhile, in August 1912, the Post Office tried once more to get a winter mailing system arranged for St Kilda. Tenders were invited, with the following replies:

Steam drifter from Stornoway £25–£30 a trip
Sailing packet from Dunvegan £25 a trip
Sailing boat from Scalpay £20 a trip

The St Kildans, however, did not want a sailing boat to take the risk, and anyway the Post Office considered the tenders far too high. Once again the Fleetwood trawlers were approached. Of the two companies invited to tender, Messrs Kelly said that they had no trawlers fishing in that area and Kelsalls asked for £10

The whaler *St Kilda*, 1917. Among the few vessels to visit St Kilda regularly during the war years was this aptly named whaler and her sister ship *Southern Breeze* which operated from Loch Bunaveneader in Harris. Note the whale lashed to the side of the ship, the lookout's crow's nest and the harpoon gun in the bows.

a trip. It should be noted that there was no connection between Kelsall Bros (whose trawlers, mistaken for Japanese gunboats, were attacked by the Russians on the Dogger Bank in October 1904) and Charles Kelsall, the eccentric bachelor (1782–1857) whose will laid the foundations for the Kelsall Fund which benefited the St Kildans in the late-nineteenth century. Though Kelsall Bros subsequently reduced their demands to £5, their offer was unacceptable to the Post Office. In desperation the Post Office turned to the Aberdeen trawlers yet again. Only one skipper could be found who took mails to St Kilda, whose habit it had been to call there on a Sunday. He would not fish on the Sabbath but took the opportunity to attend the service in St Kilda's church instead.

The Post Office made enquiries of four Aberdeen companies in the autumn of 1912. Their replies were, in the words of a Post Office official, 'the statements of business men, keen in commercial life, but quite alive to the [Post Office] Department's endeavours to serve the island'. He added that Bookless Bros' naive statement was 'almost an appeal to have the run of the inshore fishing of the island'.

Eventually, St Kilda mail was sent to Lochmaddy and despatched by the *Southern Breeze* or the *St Kilda*, two Norwegian whalers operating from the whaling station at Loch Bunaveneader in Harris. These ships often towed their catch into Village Bay where they were fastened to a buoy before being cut up and stowed in the holds. Photographs in the author's collection, taken by a seaman in 1916, reveals that this industry carried on right through the war.

Inflated whales in Village Bay. The whaling vessels were operated by a Norwegian company which regularly used the anchorage at St Kilda to strip the carcasses and store them before making the crossing back to Harris. The size of the whale can be gauged by the man perched on one of its fins.

Then, in the winter of 1912, there was an unforeseen change in the movements of the fish. Roker, grey skate, hake, ling, gurnards and codlings began to frequent the St Kilda grounds again and attracted the Fleetwood trawlers back. This gave rise to the roundabout situation where mail which had been sent to Lochmaddy from Aberdeen for St Kilda was recalled to Aberdeen and sent from there to Fleetwood to connect with Kelsall's trawler *City of York* (Captain Pedersen) on 18 September. Not surprisingly, the mail reached Fleetwood too late, and the trawler left port without it.

The Post Office also approached the Fishery Board. They replied that their vessels were not large or strong enough to go to St Kilda (though it should be remembered that the *Minna* had been able to do so and catch trawlers napping), and suggested that the Post Office try the Northern Lighthouse Commissioners. These gentlemen quoted their previous letters of 1906 and 1903 and stated that the additional steaming from the Flannans to St Kilda would cost £15.

Somehow, in spite of intransigence from other Government departments, the Post Office managed to get the mails to St Kilda during the winter of 1912–13, until the *Dunara Castle* paid her first visit of the summer on 12 June. The *Dunara* brought not only the mail but also a less welcome visitor – influenza. The St Kildans had always been prone to attacks of the common cold after a ship had called, but this proved to be a serious epidemic which prostrated the entire village by the following week. On 15 June the Hull trawler *Mercury* visited St Kilda and found twenty children seriously ill, all the women helpless and the islanders almost starving. They appealed to William Rilatt, the trawler's skipper, to send a telegram from Harris to the *Daily Mirror* as they were sure that worthy newspaper would soon stir up the authorities.

The *Daily Mirror* responded nobly, contacted the Admiralty, and, when that body appeared to be dilatory, whisked a reporter and photographer off to Glasgow, chartered the tug *Flying Serpent*, the fastest on the Clyde, and began arrangements for another relief expedition. The Admiralty, however, despatched HMS *Active* from Lamlash, Arran, on 21 June. This ship was only commissioned in 1911 and attached to the Cruiser Squadron in the Firth of Clyde, the leading ship in her class of scout cruisers. Built at Pembroke, she had a gross tonnage of 4,000, a top speed of 25 knots, and a principal armament consisting of ten 4in guns. She also had the distinctive 'ram' bow. She had a crew of 321 and, on the outbreak of war was transferred to the second Destroyer Flotilla at Harwich. She survived Jutland but was scrapped in 1920. Her dash to St Kilda saved the *Daily Mirror* considerable expense, but gave the newspaper some nicely timed publicity for its wireless station, which was shipped to St Kilda on 7 July.

The equipment, consisting of a 1.5kW petrol motor generator and a standard 10in coil transmitter with a range of 75 miles, was furnished by the Marconi Wireless Telegraph Co. and installed for the *Daily Mirror* by the London building contractors, Messrs Kilby & Gayford Ltd, whose foreman, Frederick H. Dexter, superintended the erection. They arrived at St Kilda on 10 July and the station was completed on 22 July. Dudley Ward-Millar, of the British Telegraph Instruments Co., tested the transmitter and instructed Calum MacArthur, the missionary, in how to operate it. The first messages were sent early in the morning of 29 July to King George V, the *Daily Mirror*, and J.M. Hogge MP, the Liberal member for East Edinburgh, who had taken a keen interest in the St Kildans' welfare.

A metal plate was fixed to one of the 75ft aerial masts, with the following inscription: 'This wireless station was installed by the *Daily Mirror* for the use of the inhabitants of St Kilda in time of acute distress – July 1913.' No trace of this plate or its mast now remains, but the concrete base of the mast can still be seen near the factor's house. The initials of the nine workmen and the date were scratched in the wet concrete and exist to this day.

The radio was installed in the room of the factor's house which had served as the post office, while the generator was housed in a shed nearby. The two masts were 75ft high and 150ft apart. The call-sign TDM was used, being the initials of the newspaper which had done so much to give St Kilda telegraphic communication. The post office was now moved to a corrugated iron shack adjoining cottage No.5 (Neil Ferguson's house), in order to make room for the transmitter, and here it remained until long after the evacuation of the island.

On 1 August Mr Hogge asked the Secretary of State for Scotland to secure periodic reports as to the condition of affairs on St Kilda. Now that wireless communication had been established this seemed an easy matter. By 6 October, however, the wireless station had broken down, on account of the lack of technical skill on the part of the missionary and Neil Ferguson. The *Daily Mirror* made some improvements, and a professional wireless engineer, a German called Gustaf Flick, was sent out to operate it. It later transpired that Flick was an officer in German Naval Intelligence, and information he passed to his masters in Kiel was later blamed for the bombardment of St Kilda in May 1918. Flick apparently emigrated to Australia in the 1920s.

The station communicated with Malin Head radio on a frequency of 600m for several months during the winter of 1913–14 and telegrams were sent at the normal inland rate. It was as a result of a wireless signal that a Nurse Robertson was despatched to St Kilda in January 1914 to treat an ulcerated leg. This minor mercy mission entailed a hazardous voyage from Breascleit in Lewis aboard the lighthouse steamer *Polestar* whose captain allowed her barely ninety minutes ashore to diagnose the trouble and treat the patient, Widow Macdonald. The nurse commiserated with the young German engineer who had been hard at work for several weeks but now, having repaired the radio transmitter, managed to cadge a lift on the *Polestar*: 'I never saw such joy in my life as in that boy's face when he got off the island.'

On 21 May 1914 the *Dunara Castle* made her first trip of the season, bringing out Mrs Margaret E. MacLennan, a widow who was also a trained nurse. With her came Alexander MacKinnon, the new missionary, and his wife Mary. Both nurse and missionary remained on St Kilda until the end of the First World War. Both the *Dunara* and the *Hebrides* made their usual tourist cruises to the island that summer, and on 10 July the latter ship brought out the usual delegation from the United Free Church to perform the annual Communion. On this occasion they were headed by the Rev. Dr George Reith, the moderator of the United Free Church, the first (and only) time that St Kilda received a visit from the head of their church. Dr Reith was accompanied by his eldest son, the Rev. Douglas Reith, the Rev. Alexander Lee (secretary of the Highland Committee) and W.P. Livingstone, editor of the *Missionary Record* which duly published a full account of the proceedings. The Rev. Dr Reith of Stonehaven had six children and then, after a gap of ten years, his wife bore him another son, John, destined to become Lord Reith, founder of the British Broadcasting Corporation.

The ship's purser sent his usual telegram to the *Glasgow Herald* which noted that Alexander Gillies Ferguson was also on St Kilda and had caught a greater shearwater. This very rare bird was in poor shape but 'when set up the bird will probably find a welcome at the Museum in Kelvingrove'. The *Hebrides* made one more visit, on Thursday 23 July, but the scheduled August sailings to St Kilda were suspended due to the outbreak of war.

On 5 April 1914 the *Daily Mirror* contacted the Post Office intimating that they now wished to dispose of their plant and asked if the postal authorities would take it over. The Post Office declined unless a guarantor could be found to pay, for twenty-one years, the difference between the annual cost of working and maintenance, and the receipts from telegrams handed in at St Kilda. The Scottish Office was also approached about participating in the scheme, but they refused. The Post Office estimated that the cost of operating the station was £400 a year, whereas the receipts scarcely amounted to a few pounds.

The Marconi Co. was then approached by the Post Office, since they actually owned the plant, and they considered selling it to the lessees, the *Daily Mirror*, for £350. The *Daily Mirror* thought this too much, now that St Kilda was no longer of much news value, and started to dismantle the station as early as March. In August, Marconi submitted an estimate of the annual cost of operation as £400, which could be reduced if a St Kildan could be trained properly to operate it. The Post Office accepted this offer and agreed to buy the plant for £350 if a guarantor for £200 a year could be found, and if arrangements could be made to train an islander who would operate the station unpaid. The cost of the six months training, estimated at £100, was to be borne by the guarantor.

Unhappily no guarantor could be found and so the station was closed down and partly dismantled. It seemed as though the St Kildans were to be returned to the state of isolation they had endured up until the previous winter. The outbreak of the First World War gave their wireless station a reprieve. On 5 November the Admiralty asked the Marconi Co. to re-open the station. The Post Office agreed in principle but nothing further was done until January 1915, when the Admiralty sent a naval detachment to St Kilda to man the station. St Kilda now became a War Signal Station under the Naval Centre at Aultbea.

The party, consisting of Capt. Frank Athow, Royal Marine Light Infantry (Retired), two petty officers, twelve ratings and a Marine batman, arrived at St Kilda on 12 January on board the armed trawler *Amsterdam*. Athow, though he had been on the retired list since the Boer War and had no knowledge of wireless, succeeded in getting the *Daily Mirror* set working again, with the Admiralty's portable ½kW field set as a spare, by mid-February. The Admiralty set had a range of less than 10 miles on 'Q' tune and was quite unsuitable. Even the *Mirror* set had difficulty in communicating with Lochboisdale, but at night easily contacted Malin Head. Athow left St Kilda on 20 May by steam drifter for Oban, being replaced as detachment commander by a warrant telegraphist.

During the war sailings by the *Dunara Castle*, *Hebridean* and *Hebrides* were severely curtailed. To be sure, the ships of John McCallum and Martin Orme continued to operate their normal coastal service, and on several occasions ventured out of the Sound of Harris to travel north to Loch Roag on the west coast of Lewis, but in 1915 none dared risk the voyage across 50 miles of open Atlantic to St Kilda, in waters which were infested with German submarines. Steamer posters for the war period indicate that the steamers made round trips from Glasgow and Greenock every ten days, regularly visiting Portaskaig (Islay), Colonsay, Oban, Tobermory, Coll, Tiree, then Elgol, Soay, Carbost, Colbost and Dunvegan on Skye before crossing the Minch to Lochmaddy. That was normally as far as they travelled, before heading south via Scotvin (Kallin), Carnan, Skipport and Lochboisdale (South Uist), then Castlebay (Barra) before recrossing the Minch to Tiree, Coll and all points south. By that time John McCallum and Co. had their premises at 87 Union Street, Glasgow.

If the coastal steamers gave St Kilda a wide berth during the first year of the war, the island was actually far less isolated than it ever was, before or since. The personnel of the tiny garrison was changed every four months, being originally supplied and provisioned from HMS *Cyclops* at Scapa Flow. This arrangement soon proved unwieldy and responsibility for St Kilda was transferred to the Rear Admiral, Stornoway. From July 1915 until the end of the war the garrison was victualled and supplied by HM Depot Ship *Manco*, based at Stornoway, whither the Naval Centre had been transferred earlier that year.

During the summer of 1915 neither the *Hebrides* nor *Dunara Castle* visited St Kilda, and sailings by these cargo vessels were not in fact resumed to the island until July 1916 when a modified service was introduced. On the other hand St Kilda now came into the area patrolled by ten armed trawlers and several armed whalers based on Stornoway, and these gave the island a weekly mail service both summer and winter throughout the war.

Above: SS *Hebrides* in Loch Dunvegan, 1916. During the First World War the movement of this steamer was restricted owing to submarine activity in the waters around St Kilda.

Right: Warship in Village Bay, 1916. It may have been HMS *Manco* which was the flagship of the rear admiral commanding the naval base at Stornoway, and which visited the island on several occasions. This was one of several photographs taken by a naval rating, James Pirie, who served on St Kilda during the First World War.

Naval officer on the jetty,
1916. According to a pencil
annotation by James Pirie,
this was Rear Admiral Tupper
who took a keen interest in
this tiny naval outpost. The
admiral is shown conversing
with some of the island girls
on the jetty.

They included the armed trawlers *Ophir*, *Lacerta*, *East Coast*, *Sasebo*, and many others, which are discussed more fully in my book *Soldiering on St Kilda* (2001). From time to time these ships were supplemented by visits from cruisers of the Grand Fleet such as HMS *Alsatian* and *Calyx*. All mail for St Kilda came and went via Stornoway and from 1915 to 1919 the postal address of the island was designated: 'St Kilda, Stornoway, Isle of Lewis.' Its telegraphic address, however, was styled: 'St Kilda, Lochboisdale, South Uist.' Although the sub-post office on the island continued to function, mail from St Kilda at the end of the war and even into 1919 and 1920 has been recorded bearing Stornoway or Oban postmarks.

At 10.40 a.m. on 15 May 1918 a German submarine surfaced in Village Bay and shelled the village, demolishing the store house and severely damaging the manse, church, two cottages and the wireless station, which was briefly put out of action. The islanders took refuge in the Dry Burn, a deep gully behind the village and, although seventy-two rounds were fired, no-one was injured. The radio was subsequently repaired, and a 4in Mk III QF gun on PI mounting was erected in late October for the defence of the island. The station was dismantled at the end of the war and the naval detachment was withdrawn on 6 February 1919.

Neil Ferguson added to his multifarious duties as postmaster, ground officer and kirk elder the new appointment of custodian of the gun. For a year or two he received the sum of £25 annually to maintain and clean the gun. 'Then the Admiralty stopped the payments so Father stopped greasing the Gun', his son recalled many years later. The gun and its nearby underground magazine remain near the store house to this day. Its breech-block was removed in 1919 and its whereabouts were unknown until the summer of 1962 when it was uncovered among the rocks near the jetty where it had lain undamaged for more than forty years. The gun itself had become rusty with decades of neglect and had been slewed round so that its muzzle pointed at the church. But in the 1960s the Royal Artillery garrison winched it round to face out to sea, removed the rust and painted it, giving it a tolerably serviceable appearance.

Eight

Decline and Fall

With the departure of the Navy, St Kilda returned to normal. The *Dunara Castle* and *Hebrides* resumed their full programme of visits in the summer of 1919. The war had left its mark on St Kilda nevertheless, and was the main factor contributing to the ultimate evacuation eleven years later. Apart from greatly enhanced communications the St Kildans were allowed to travel free of charge on the naval vessels that called in at Village Bay several times a week from their base at Stornoway. However, this all came to an abrupt end on 6 February 1919 when the Navy men were withdrawn.

Like many other places, St Kilda enjoyed during the war a measure of prosperity unparalleled before and never attained after. For the first time the islanders were independent of the system of barter with their proprietor, and money circulated freely on the island. Not only did they receive on numerous occasions free food supplies from the Navy, but most of the men were enrolled at 2s a day as watchers to man the lookout posts set up on Conachair, Oiseval and Mullach Mòr. In addition several of them were paid half a crown a day for digging trenches, erecting huts for the sailors' accommodation and laying telephone cables. One sailor married a St Kilda girl and settled down there briefly after the war, but the influence of the Navy caused the drift in the opposite direction. Attracted by visions of greater prosperity on the mainland many of the island's young people left St Kilda in 1919 and 1920. In these years the population fell by more than 25 per cent.

Up to the end of the nineteenth century the economy of St Kilda was very largely based on seabirds and such by-products as fulmar oil and feathers, the latter in great demand for feather mattresses. By 1900 there was little demand for feathers and by 1920 it had vanished altogether. In the same period the main commodity produced by the St Kildans was tweed, hand-woven over the winter months. Up to 1900, the sole conduit for this material was the factor, John Mackenzie, who sold it on the islanders' behalf to MacFarlan, Shearer & Co. of Greenock at 1*s* 9*d* a web (about 28 yards), yielding in 1900 a grand total of £48 4*s* 2*d* – rather less than the St Kildans earned in direct sales to the tourists off the steamers. Writing in 1928, the geographer John Mathieson estimated that the St Kildans annually produced 1,000 to 1,200 yards of hand-woven tweed, most of it sold to the tourists off the steamers. St Kilda tweed was inferior in quality to Harris tweed and much more expensive. It was purchased out of sentiment for its novelty, but it depended almost entirely on the chance impulse of an uncertain market.

After 1900, of course, as Alexander Ferguson took over the role of the factor and the middle-man, the actual net value of St Kilda tweed rose considerably. After the war, a new aspect of trading was provided by mail order. The St Kildans were beginning to develop direct sales to customers on the mainland. Presumably this began through contact with the excursionists who, satisfied with the purchases made during their summer visits, desired repeat orders, and then the practice expanded by word of mouth. Neil MacKinnon, for example, was sending swatches of tweed to potential customers from September 1919 onwards, and quoting prices of 8*s* 6*d* or 9*s* a yard, depending on colour – a far cry from the 3 farthings a yard netted twenty years earlier. Such mail order business would have been impossible in earlier decades but it was made possible by the extension of the parcel post to St Kilda after the sub-post office opened, and the use of postal orders for remittances, the sale or encashment of which only became possible at St Kilda from April 1904 onwards. What had been a barter economy at subsistence level since time immemorial had, as a result of the war, become a cash economy, dependent on pounds, shillings and pence for a wide range of luxuries undreamed of a few years earlier.

The submarine bombardment not only destroyed the islanders' store house but also their two best boats. Because they had not availed themselves of the Governmental Insurance Scheme no compensation was paid to them, and although the island would have been unmolested had a naval wireless station not existed there, the Admiralty stated in a letter to the factor, John Mackenzie, as late as April 1919 that it was 'not concerned in the matter'. The only person who received any compensation was Nurse Gillon, who had succeeded Mrs

MacLennan in 1916 and lived on the island until 1919. She received £20 from the Board of Health (her employers) for the loss of medicines and equipment when the rooms she occupied on the ground floor of the factor's house took a direct hit. The factor's house was repaired in the spring of 1919 and made habitable in time for the arrival of the next nurse, Mrs J.M. Mackenzie, whose term continued until the summer of 1923, when she was replaced by Nurse MacDougall. Neither the store house nor the first cottage in the street were repaired before the evacuation; ironically, both have been restored in recent years as part of the conservation programme carried out by the National Trust for Scotland. From 1920 onwards there was a steady drain of St Kildans leaving the island, attracted by the lure of the mainland. At first they left in ones and twos, but the departure of the Macdonald family en masse was a devastating blow to the morale of those left behind. The population gradually declined to forty-five in 1927 and thirty-six in 1930, by which time there were scarcely sufficient able-bodied men left to man the St Kilda boat and evacuation became imperative.

By 1919 the Aberdeen and Fleetwood trawlers had returned to their old fishing grounds. Occasional notices in the *Glasgow Herald* or *The Scotsman* intimated that a trawler would be leaving one of these ports with the intention of calling at St Kilda and consequently giving the latest times of posting letters at Glasgow or Edinburgh to connect with the departure of that vessel. The mail arrangements during the winter of 1919–20 were erratic; bags were sent from Fleetwood and Inverness, and the payment to trawlers for carrying the mail was still fixed at £1 for the round trip. When Lord Provost Stewart of Glasgow sent a 'memorial' to the Post Office in January 1920, urging a more regular and frequent communication with St Kilda, he was informed that a regular service had been inaugurated from Fleetwood and that, as a result, mails had been delivered at St Kilda on 9 and 30 December 1919.

Neil Ferguson got a slight pay rise in 1920. By 1926 it reached its maximum of £15 4s, plus a bonus of £10 13s ferriage, while delivery money, which he also received in his dual capacity as boatman and postman, now amounted in that year to £8 19s 4d.

The nineteenth century tradition of ships calling at St Kilda on their maiden voyages was upheld in 1923. On 9 June the pride of the Blue Funnel Line, the SS *Sarpedon* (named after the son of Zeus and Laodamia) left Liverpool on her maiden voyage, bound for the Far East. She was built by Cammell Laird of Birkenhead and launched on 2 February 1923. She had a gross tonnage of 11,321 and was essentially a cargo vessel, but she was also the first of her kind to have substantial passenger accommodation and, between 1946 and 1953, when she was scrapped, she carried thousands of British migrants to Australia. On her maiden voyage she had a crew of eighty and about 150 passengers on board. Although her destination was Singapore, she first headed north and, apparently more by chance than deliberate intent, called at St Kilda where the captain found the islanders completely out of flour, meal and sugar. A substantial quantity of these and other foodstuffs was put ashore, and tided the St Kildans over until the arrival of the *Hebrides* a few days later on her first cruise of the season.

In the early 1920s a fairly regular mail service was maintained in winter between St Kilda and Fleetwood. Mary Cameron, daughter of Donald Cameron (missionary 1919–26), said that she once counted no fewer than forty-seven trawlers sheltering in Village Bay. The principal mail trawler in this period was the *Erna* (FD 158) which carried mail almost exclusively until September 1924. In this period the skipper was Tommy Sandham whose photograph, seated on the steps of the post office on Sunday 13 July 1924, with Arthur Ramsay of Manchester, was captioned on the back: 'Closed for the Sabbath.' Ramsay was an official of the Post Office surveyor's department and may have been on this voyage to observe the working of the winter mail arrangements.

Tommy sent a print of this photograph to Charlie Brewster, a fellow trawlerman, on 10 January 1925 from his home at Milton Street, Fleetwood. The covering letter is not without interest for its comments on the current state of an island which was so familiar to both of them. The *Erna*, in fact, had just returned from a mid-winter voyage:

Oh what a longing I had for home this time, not half. You will remember 'Soay Stack' [one of the St Kilda rocks], well on Xmas Eve a gale sprang up and of course we made a dash for Finlay's home [Finlay McQueen] in the snow and we got the worse shaking up with the backwash from the Stack any ship ever had, and we were the means of saving 9 or 10 ships from coming to grief by keeping near the stack and blowing our whistle until they were all safely under shelter and we then were guided by their lights to our own safety. That is only one little episode of the trip's duration. I could relate many others were you here and it would just simply make Iceland a passing thought I'm sure and no kid about it. Oh, by the way Charlie, Bessie McQueen has gone into service in Glasgow, and also two other families have really forsaken their 'Lil Old Home' for Leverburgh in the Isle of Lewis [Obbe in Harris actually] not far from Stornoway.

I'm sure you must have been very busy these holidays and I'm sure you will not be sorry when it is all over. But your hours have been short to mine this last 16 days I assure you, in fact once I had 2 hours sleep one day without any interruption can you beat it, and we had no down anchor although we did lay under the lea of Kilda's…

Right: Tommy Sandham (skipper of trawler *Erna*) and Arthur Ramsay of Manchester PO, sitting on the steps of the post office on a Sunday in July 1924. Sandham was one of several trawler skippers who took a keen personal interest in the welfare of the islanders.

Below: The Fleetwood trawler *Erna*, a regular caller at St Kilda throughout the 1920s, providing a measure of communications at a time when official contact with the island was meagre.

From the end of 1924 until the spring of 1926 the trawlers *Philip Godby*, *Osprey*, *Thomas Leeds*, and *Alberia* took the mails to St Kilda, and others, including the *Caldew* and the *Gaul*, brought mail back to Fleetwood. Occasionally the whalers *Southern Breeze* and *St Kilda* took mail from the island to Harris; it was the least they could do, for the islanders had to tolerate the stink of the whales, inflated and tethered to a buoy in Village Bay, until the whalers could transport them to Harris for processing.

The arrival of a trawler was always a cause for excitement and anticipation on St Kilda – perhaps there would be a mailbag if they were lucky, or at least some newspapers no more than a few days old. One day in May 1926, Neil Ferguson Junior and some of the other men rowed out to a trawler which lay at anchor, but as they approached a crew member warned them not to come aboard as several of the crew were laid low with influenza. Heedless of the warning, the St Kildans clambered aboard to pick up newspapers. Within days, the entire population – always prone to infection brought by visiting ships – was confined to bed. Even Nurse Littlejohn was too ill to attend the stricken islanders. Eventually some of the men managed to struggle to the summit of Conachair and lit a fire, hoping to attract some passing ship, but none appeared. The epidemic carried off four of the elderly inhabitants. On the evening of the day that the last of the victims was laid to rest in the tiny cemetery the *Hebrides* made her inaugural run of the season, bringing urgently needed supplies of food and medicines, both of which had virtually run out.

Although the St Kildans eventually recovered from the physical effects of the epidemic, the 'flu had dealt their corporate morale a shattering blow, and the pace of emigration accelerated thereafter. It was exacerbated by new problems over winter communications on which the St Kildans had come to rely so much in recent years. When the winter service was resumed on 7 September 1926 only one trawler, the *Robert Murray* (master Sidney A. Tonner), would undertake to carry mail to and from St Kilda. Nevertheless, mail was despatched to and from the island by this trawler once a month, on average, in the winters of 1926 and 1927. Even provisions and passengers were carried to St Kilda. By this means, the geographers John Mathieson and A.M. Cockburn were enabled to visit St Kilda on 19 April 1927, returning to the mainland the following September aboard the Aberdeen trawler *Ugiebank*.

Sidney Tonner now began to feel that 10s each way was insufficient recompense. In January 1928 he wrote to the postmaster of Fleetwood asking for £5 a round trip. He stated that on his last trip on 6 December bad weather delayed the landing and lost him two tides which meant a loss of £50 in steaming costs. The Post Office stood firm on the principle that the £1 it now paid was merely a token of their appreciation for services rendered and nothing more.

As a result Tonner did not take mail to St Kilda in 1928. He changed his fishing ground and later had an accident which put him in hospital for several months. St Kilda was therefore cut off for eleven weeks, being relieved eventually at the end of February 1929 by the trawler *Loughrig* which took eleven sacks of mail from Fleetwood.

In the winter of 1928 an attempt to send the mail via Aberdeen was only partially successful. Two despatches were made in November by the *Strath Atholl*, whose skipper, Albert Walkner, it will be remembered, had been fined for poaching round St Kilda two decades earlier. The owners were annoyed when they found that Walkner had taken the mail and forbade its continuance. Donald Craig, skipper of the *John Gillman*, was willing to deliver mail, but the owner, R.W. Lewis, opposed it.

In summertime, the pleasure steamers returned with their full complement of tourists. Although the *Dunara Castle* generally had the reputation of being a lucky ship, she did suffer a few accidents. The most serious of these occurred in August 1922 when she ran on to the rocks at Battery Point, Greenock, but was re-floated without serious damage. In 1923 the *Hebrides* brought to St Kilda a camera crew led by Paul Robello and Bobbie Mann who spent several days on the island making a film which was eventually released five years later under the title of *St Kilda, Britain's Loneliest Isle*. The film was made by Topical Productions as a promotional film for John McCallum and was given a screening in many of the cinemas in and around Glasgow, a city perceived by the shipping company as their main customer base. The silent movie, shot in black and white, conveyed the drama of St Kilda, and included a focus on its breathtaking scenery, offered some quite candid shots of the St Kildans, and looked at the voyage itself all the way from Glasgow. It gained added poignancy as, within two years of its general release, St Kilda had become a desert isle.

Several scenes showed island women and girls, heads covered in plaid shawls, eyeing the camera with amazement and curiosity or scurrying away to hide from it, giving the impression that they had never seen a camera before. These scenes were obviously staged by the cameraman. In fact, the first professional film was shot as long ago as 1908 by Oliver Pike, and countless photographs from 1860 onwards show that the St Kildans were no strangers to the camera. Several other films exist from the 1920s but these were 'home movies' made by passengers and the quality is variable. Stills from this film were subsequently made into a series of picture postcards and also a set of twelve small photographs which were sold on board the steamers during their frequent cruises to the 'desert isle' in the 1930s.

A cigarette card in the 1920s series published by Mitchell's of Glasgow illustrating river and coastal steamers of Scotland. Both the *Hebrides* and the *Dunara* Castle were featured in this series.

The *Dunara Castle* at Dunvegan, Isle of Skye, in the 1920s, clearly showing the primitive, often makeshift docking facilities at most of the little ports of the West Highlands and Islands.

The steamer companies seem to have acted in concert latterly. Both of them produced new brochures in 1925 which were remarkably similar in appearance. Both advertised their cruises to St Kilda, the price for the basic round trip being pegged at the pre-war level of £10. Allowing for some inflation since 1914 this was remarkably good value for money but, despite some refurbishment, the steamers, especially the *Dunara Castle* (now fifty years old), were showing their age.

On 20 August 1926 the *Hebrides* called at St Kilda on what should have been her last visit of the season, but was unable to land the mails and the vast quantity of stores required to sustain the island over the coming winter. A dangerous south-easterly storm sprang up with ferocious suddenness shortly after the vessel anchored in Village Bay that afternoon, forcing her to weigh anchor and steam round to Glen Bay, but as the storm showed no sigh of abating and kept fluctuating in strength and direction, the steamer headed out into the comparative safety of the open Atlantic and then returned to the Sound of Harris and all points south. In mid-September the whaler *Southern Breeze* called at the island and subsequently raised the alarm that the St Kildans were on the verge of starvation and in a very desperate situation.

John McCallum & Co. had already decided to attempt one last trip to St Kilda before the winter closed in, but news of the island's distress hitting the headlines clinched the matter. The *Hebrides*, laden with the undelivered stores, set out from Glasgow on 16 September and reached the island on Monday, three days later. In fact, the bulk of provisions for the coming winter had already been delivered by the *Dunara Castle* in mid-August, leaving the *Hebrides* to take out a cargo which consisted mainly of coal for the missionary, John MacLeod (who had just taken over from Donald Cameron, who had ministered to the little congregation since 1919) together with some provisions for two widows consigned through the generosity of Sir Reginald MacLeod the proprietor, and 'some odd things' for Nurse Littlejohn who had been in residence since the previous year.

The *Glasgow Herald* sent a special correspondent on this voyage and he duly provided a very full report which was published on Friday 24 September under the headline 'ST KILDA NO PROSPECT OF DISTRESS', with the sub-heading 'PLIGHT OF INHABITANTS EXAGGERATED'. Apart from setting readers' minds at rest regarding the condition of St Kilda, the article was chiefly of interest for the comments on the population, which now consisted of forty-three natives and five incomers, made up of the missionary, his wife and two children, and the nurse. The island's natural resources, with their wealth of bird life and excellent grazing for sheep and cattle, made the islanders infinitely better off than in many parts of the Western Isles. Poverty on St Kilda 'can never be so bad as I have seen in Lewis, Harris and other parts of the Western Highlands', wrote the correspondent. However, he got to the root of the problem:

> Contact with an urbanised civilisation, however, has expanded the wants of the islanders. They import tea, sugar, jam, flour and other commodities for which, when payment is necessary, they pay with their wool and tweeds and 'pickings' from visitors. They grow on their crofts comparatively good crops of oats, barley and potatoes. The St Kildans pay no rates and no taxes and only one pays his rent. At a pinch they could subsist without imports – which is more than can be said for the United Kingdom as a whole.

The writer maintained that the St Kildans were trading on the interest of the mainland: 'The isolation of St Kilda in the stormy North Atlantic… its bleakness and the vestiges of the primitive in the inhabitants, all combine to stir the memories of a race whose adventures still throw a shadow across its sophisticated routine ways.'

By contrast with the 'shawlies' of the 1923 promotional film, most photographs of islanders in the 1920s show them to have been remarkably well dressed by that period, indeed, one might almost say, in the height of fashion, the women in particular sporting bobbed hair, cloche hats and short skirts – a far cry from the severe hairstyles and ankle-length homespuns of the late Victorian and Edwardian period.

The anonymous correspondent regretted that sentiment should effervesce into sentimentality: 'The main trouble with the St Kildans is the fuss that is made over them. It hurts both them and us. Hundreds of children die unnecessarily in the slums of Glasgow and their deaths pass almost unnoticed, but an epidemic of a slight and common infection in St Kilda may light a flare of public sentiment on the mainland that is not put out until a medical team have landed on the island and reported all well.' The St Kildans had come to expect this interest and, not surprisingly, they traded on it. The influenza outbreak earlier that summer might be inconsequential to someone writing in Glasgow, but undoubtedly it was the turning point on deciding the fate of the little community.

In fact, the journalist defended the St Kildans against the charge of begging from the tourists. Visitors to the island were, quite naturally, fair game and, indeed, they had inculcated this by their distribution of largesse which was regarded as *de rigueur*. 'They ask readily for things they lack and give readily to those in need. It is necessary for civilised people to be chary of moral judgments on this primitive communism.'

He maintained that the St Kildans were still gripped 'by joyless religious forms' and did not dance or play musical instruments – 'there is not even a mouth organ or tin whistle on the island' – but he added that there was now a gramophone on St Kilda. During a cruise of the *Hebrides* in 1911 one of the passengers had brought ashore a gramophone with a large horn and there are photographs showing women with their knitting-needles clacking away as they listen to the music. The *Herald* writer hinted that St Kilda was about to get a wireless set. The primitive radio station of 1913–19 was only capable of transmitting and receiving Morse signals, but, in fact, a wireless set was installed in the home of Neil Ferguson in 1927. The last photographs of the post office prior to the evacuation show the mast and aerial which presumably enabled the Fergusons (and their neighbours) to listen to the BBC broadcasts via the Malin Head transmitter in Northern Ireland. Whether the St Kildans ever danced to the music of the Savoy Band brought over the airwaves is debatable.

Having conceded that he found the St Kildans had a sense of humour, nearly all spoke English and had 'a quickness of intelligence that is rare enough in the cities', he could not resist falling into the trap of instant judgment based on hackneyed prejudice: 'But generally they are a ragged lot, ragged and excitable. Their excited jabber in Gaelic, their gesticulations and fecklessness as they board the steamer and carry out the business of landing passengers and cargo, is a unique thing, to my knowledge, in the British Isles.'

House No. 5 (occupied by Neil Ferguson and his family), with the corrugated iron shack which had served as the post office since 1913. Note the wireless mast at the side; the Fergusons boasted the only wireless receiver on the island but there had been no transmitter since 1919. This photograph, taken on 25 August 1930, shows some of the passengers from the *Dunara Castle* buying souvenirs. Note also the paved 'street' and the gables of the 1830 'black houses' between the 1860 houses.

Colin Macdonald, himself a Gaelic speaker, wrote several volumes of memoirs and, in one of these, entitled *Suil Air Ais* ('Looking Back') he recounted a visit to St Kilda in the 1920s. Being rowed ashore by the St Kildans one of the lady passengers asked the boatman how much he was charging to take her. The boatman appeared to squint up at the sky while he discussed the fare in Gaelic with his companions, concluding that he would ask 'the ugly one' for a shilling. The lady, herself a Gael, retorted sharply in the same language: 'I may be ugly, but I'm not stupid. I will pay you twopence, same as everyone else!' Latterly, however, a shilling was the standard tariff for the experience of being taken ashore in one of the St Kildan boats; the longboats lowered by the steamers presumably carried passengers at no extra charge.

The *Glasgow Herald* article of 1926 followed the customary formula, ending with the usual speculation on the island's future: 'Possibly St Kilda will follow Mingulay and other islands in the Hebrides, as well as parts of the mainland in the Highlands. If so, the population will continue to decline, through emigration and death, until the island is left once more to animal life.' However, he did not advocate evacuation as a matter of course: 'The St Kildans get a living, a bare one, but they get it easily – a fact which explains the common accusation against them that they are lazy… The fate of St Kilda will be determined by chance and the spirit of man.'

In 1927–9 the *Dunara Castle* and the *Hebrides* paid four visits apiece. Travelling on the *Dunara* in June 1927, on the steamer's first voyage of the summer, was Seton Gordon from Duntulm in northern Skye, who boarded at Uig. He was a kenspeckle figure who invariably wore a kilt (which must have been an interesting sight for the St Kildans) and was one of Scotland's foremost naturalists. He wrote twenty-seven books about his travels around the Highlands and, in *Isles of the West* (published in 1933), he gave an absorbing account of his visit to St Kilda. Strangely enough, he got the date wrong, saying that he had been there in 1928; as he recounted his experiences in a series of articles which appeared under his name in the *Glasgow Herald* – an introductory feature (1 July), a visit to Boreray (23 July) and the epic ascent of the cliffs on Soay (30 July) – there can be no doubt that the year was 1927.

He was fortunate to be on the island at a time when Mathieson and Cockburn were spending their first season there, carrying out a detailed survey of the archipelago, and thus it was that he was able to accompany them on visits to Borerary and Soay, described in breathtaking detail. Gordon disembarked from the *Dunara* on Sunday 26 June, along with the factor, John T. Mackenzie, through whose hospitality he was able to stay at the factor's house during his sojourn. While Nurse Littlejohn was accommodated in one of the rooms downstairs, Mathieson and Cockburn had the two rooms upstairs, approached from a door at the back of the building.

He also commented on the fact that the only other vessel at anchor in Village Bay that Sunday was the trawler *Prevoyance Sociale* from Ostend, and was amazed to think that a trawler should come all the way from Belgium. It was the first recorded reference to Belgian trawlers frequenting St Kilda. Sadly, it would not be the last.

Over the years countless newspaper reports and magazine articles about St Kilda had been penned by passengers on visiting yachts and steamers. A sign of the times, however, was the reporting of conditions on the island written by George Blair, the purser of the *Hebrides*, or Mr Wylie, his counterpart on the *Dunara Castle*. These gentlemen regularly filed reports by radiotelegram to their respective owners and it was McCallum or Orme who now forwarded the latest news to *The Scotsman* and the *Glasgow Herald*. Where these reports were more dramatic than usual they were invariably reprinted with minor variations in the English press. The *Glasgow Herald*, for example, noted the arrival of one or other of the two steamers at St Kilda on 26 May, 27 June, 18 July and 18 August 1928, and on 25 May, 26 June, 17 July, 17 August 1929.

Donald John Ferguson at the post office in the summer of 1929. The son of the postmaster, he was a lighthouse keeper. This picture was subsequently published as a postcard by McCallum Orme.

Typical of these reports was the one headed 'A Boisterous Crossing' which appeared in *The Scotsman* of 26 June 1929. It dealt with the second voyage that summer of the *Hebrides* which, on leaving the Sound of Harris, ran into a fresh northerly breeze 'which let us in for a rather boisterous crossing to St Kilda. The Village Bay, however, afforded the necessary shelter for the safe landing of mails, passengers and cargo'. The report mentioned that the factor, John T. Mackenzie, was on board, making his forty-eighth annual visit. The *Hebrides* took off the resident missionary John MacLeod with his wife Katie and their four children, Donald John, Alexander, Chrissie and Kenneth, who disembarked with their personal effects at Lochmaddy. MacLeod was replaced by Dugald Munro, who arrived on St Kilda with the next trip of the *Hebrides* on 11 July. Purser Blair recorded an unusually large number of clerical gentlemen on this voyage, including Rev. A. Campbell of Luss, Rev. D.B. Baxter of Largs and Rev. T. Macdonald of Blairlogie. The ministers organised a service in the saloon on the Sabbath morning while the ship lay at anchor in Loch Dunvegan prior to the trip out to St Kilda.

Blair also noted that 'Queen's Nurse Barclay landed to take up duty after a brief holiday on the mainland'. Williamina Barclay had already spent a winter on St Kilda, having replaced Nurse Littlejohn in 1928. She would play a prominent role in the events which unfolded over the ensuing winter and culminated in the evacuation of the island.

Two events occurred in 1929 which had some impact on St Kilda. The first was a further amalgamation of religious sects. It will be remembered that the Free Church had joined with the United Presbyterian Church at the beginning of the century to form the United Free Church. Now it had joined forces with the

Paper napkin of the McCallum Orme steamers, retained by James Dryden as a souvenir of the evacuation cruise of August 1930. The two steamship companies had merged only a year before St Kilda was evacuated.

Established Church of Scotland, from which the Free Church had broken away in 1843. This union, which had been in gestation for a considerable time, was calmly accepted on St Kilda. It coincided with the departure of John MacLeod and the arrival of Dugald Munro, both of whom adhered to the union. The transition, so far as St Kilda was concerned, was smoothly undertaken, but it meant that the Church of Scotland, which had been absent from St Kilda since the departure of the Rev. Neil Mackenzie in 1844, was now in charge and in due course fell heir to the church, manse, school and all the equipment and appurtenances, from the old bell of the *Janet Cowan* (wrecked near St Kilda in 1864) that summoned the islanders to worship, to the Communion plate and tokens.

The spirit of ecumenism extended also in the shipping world and in the autumn of 1929 John McCallum and Martin Orme amalgamated to form McCallum, Orme & Co. Ltd, the main assets being the *Hebrides* and *Dunara Castle*. Prior to the amalgamation the house flags of the respective companies were blue with a thistle on a white disc and a saltire (St Andrew's cross), but from 1929 onwards the flag had a thistle in full colour superimposed on the saltire. From 1930 onwards the cruise brochures would publicise both vessels and the monthly handbills with the sailing schedules would list them side by side.

The merger was the logical outcome of many years of friendly competition and latterly contract-sharing, and it seems also to have been motivated by the upheavals which had overtaken the West Coast giant, MacBrayne, in 1927–8, losing its mail contracts because its ageing fleet could no longer cope effectively, and as a consequence teetering on the verge of bankruptcy. This had led to a rescue operation mounted by the London, Midland & Scottish Railway and Coast Lines Ltd, this vital shipping network which they now jointly owned being renamed David MacBrayne (1928) Ltd. While MacBrayne ran into serious trouble in the 1920s, the crews of the McCallum Orme ships were the envy of the West Highland trade. They worked long hours but they were the highest paid seamen and they had an *esprit de corps* that was second to none. Their skippers were real characters, fondly remembered to this day.

When the tourist season of 1929 was drawing to a close the newly arrived missionary, Dugald Munro, wrote on 10 August to Tom Johnston, the Under-Secretary of State for Scotland suggesting that the lighthouse steamers *Pharos* and *Polestar* be used to maintain regular communications over the forthcoming winter months. Meanwhile, the Air Ministry was toying with the idea of establishing a meteorological station on St Kilda but abandoned the idea at the end of September. St Kilda's plight was found to be acute when Captain Tonner, now in the trawler *Merisia*, called on 16 October to discover that no mail had been despatched since the tourist steamer had called on 15 August, and that medical supplies were now urgently required.

The Post Office communicated this information to the Board of Health for Scotland, who replied inconsequentially that, since they had not heard from the St Kilda nurse herself, the matter could not be serious, and therefore they did not propose to do anything about it. Later it was discovered that an epidemic of wet eczema had broken out on the island.

Meanwhile five bags of parcels and one bag of letters had accumulated at Fleetwood. George Stark, the head postmaster, was being hounded by freelance journalists and the local press for details of St Kilda's isolation, and the trawler owners were distinctly hostile. Stark had tried to arrange winter mails for St Kilda. He interviewed five trawler owners but none was prepared to take the mail. At one time the trawler skippers had had a measure of independence, since it was left to their own initiative to fish wherever they chose. Now, however, trawlers were fitted with radio and got their instructions after they had left port. Thus it was no longer possible to give mail to the trawlers at Fleetwood.

The skippers had no advantage now in calling at St Kilda. Formerly they had relied on hearsay information from the islanders as to the movement of fish, but now this could be supplied by radio. The gain of 10s or £1 from carrying the mail was more than offset by the £12 to £15 costs for extra steaming off course, charged before the skipper's share of the profit on the voyage was reckoned. Tonner had in fact been temporarily relieved of his command in 1927 for making too many trips to St Kilda. Moreover, the fish now most profitable in Fleetwood was hake, which feeds on the ocean bed. The seabed round St Kilda was too rocky and destructive to nets, and so the trawlers stayed away.

The Post Office asked the Board of Agriculture for Scotland to suggest an alternative but they were regretfully unable to provide one. The Fishery Board was next approached; they enquired of the Aberdeen trawling companies, but though they fished near Rockall they said they were unlikely to call at St Kilda. The Board of Health was then approached and they suggested, not very helpfully, that the Post Office should make enquiries at Aberdeen. The Northern Lighthouse Commissioners, when approached, automatically referred back to their correspondence of 1903–12.

Nevertheless, George Stark did manage by entreaty to get the skipper of the Fleetwood trawler *San Sebastian* to take the accumulated mail on 22 October. This led to considerable friction between the head postmaster and the owners of the *San Sebastian*, the Boston Deep Sea Fishing & Ice Co., who wrote to Stark:

> We should never dream of asking a postman to deliver an unstamped letter for us whilst he was on his rounds – which would be a much less expensive business than delivering mails to St Kilda as the vessel is bound to lose a lot of time in carrying out this service, especially if the weather should be stormy when he arrived at St Kilda and during a time when it would be impossible to land in a small boat.

This hostility of the trawler owners was most embarrassing to the Post Office. Stark forwarded this correspondence to Edinburgh with a bitter memorandum:

> In the past, despatches have been secured mainly by the good offices of Trawler skippers who have frequently acted in this matter in opposition to the wish of the Owners but this source of help has been lost by newspaper publicity. There are so many free-lance journalists in this town who subsist on such scraps that a sailing to St Kilda is as important as a Government defeat and is usually broadcast at once.

Dugald Munro used the *San Sebastian*'s visit as an opportunity to get off another letter on 25 October to Tom Johnston, informing him of the grave situation and lack of mail. With a touch of pathos he added: 'They, the St Kildans, are, like many of us, expecting equity and consideration from a Labour Government, that was denied them by previous administrations.'

Between that date and 15 January 1930 no mail went to, or came from, St Kilda. At last, after so many years of refusal, the Lighthouse Commissioners permitted their steamer *Hesperus* to take the mails, which had accumulated twenty bags of letters and parcels by 16 December. The *Hesperus* sailed from Oban on that date but adverse weather conditions forced her to return without landing, and the mail was sent back to Glasgow three days later. In January the trawler *Caldew* called at St Kilda on her way home to Fleetwood and found that Mary Gillies was desperately ill with appendicitis. The *Caldew* telegraphed via Malin Head to the General Post Office in Edinburgh on 30 January and on 15 February the fishery cruiser *Norna* sailed from Tarbert in Harris with mail, to bring off the sick woman. Unfortunately help was too late in coming: although she was evacuated she died two days later in Stobhill Hospital, Glasgow. The cost of despatching the *Norna* on this futile mission was estimated at £200.

Nurse Barclay took this opportunity to write to the Department of Health, warning them the situation on St Kilda had now reached a critical point. Erratic and infrequent communications resulted in periodic shortages of food. Although she did not actually say so, it was abundantly clear that a community which had been self-reliant for thousands of years, subsisting off their own crops and the seabirds, had now become so dependent on mainland foodstuffs that any disruption of services by cruise steamers or trawlers could be potentially disastrous.

Two bags of mail were landed from a Fleetwood trawler on 18 February; thereafter no further contact was made with St Kilda until 15 April when the trawler *Harry Melling* found the islanders starving and extremely despondent. The skipper, Thomas Quirk, was fishing in the vicinity of the island when he observed a rowing boat with eight men at the oars come out of the bay and approach the trawler. On board was Williamina Barclay, who told him in the strongest terms that the St Kildans were starving and appealed to him to inform 'the outer world' of their plight. Their potato crop had been ruined by frosts and the people were subsisting on 'meal and water' (porridge). Quirk's immediate response was to hand over the trawler's entire stock of potatoes and vegetables, and as many other provisions as he could spare. On return to Fleetwood, Quirk passed on this vital information to Harry Melling of 'St Kilda', Garstang Road, Fulwood, Preston, the trawler owner, and he immediately organised emergency supplies, including half a ton of potatoes and other provisions, packed tightly in the fish rooms of the trawler which was sent off the next day and reached the island on 20 April.

This latest act in the long-running drama provoked the usual press coverage. The *Daily Mail* ran a piece on 16 April under the headlines: 'RELIEF RUSHED TO ST KILDA. PEOPLE STARVING AGAIN. SHOULD ISLAND BE EVACUATED?'

The writer stated:

> The community has no object except a precarious existence on what is little more than a rock. There is no light-house on the island and the only industry – cloth weaving – produces little more than £20 a year. The living conditions on the island are deplorable and there is constant sickness. In recent years inter-marriage has been common.

Some years previously an attempt had been made to assess rates on the inhabitants but the cost of collecting the money would have far exceeded the paltry return and, in any case, it suited Inverness-shire County Council not to press the point. Asked to comment on the current situation, Lieutenant-Colonel Grant Smith of Grantown-on-Spey – about as far from St Kilda as you could get but still be in the same county – admitted that the island came within the jurisdiction of the council (of which he was a member) but added: 'The people have no service at all from the county, and I think it would be the best thing for them if they left their island.'

There was a dreary similarity between the reports and articles which appeared in the national newspapers at this time, and they were unanimous in their conclusion that the best thing now would be to clear the last remaining inhabitants off the island. The main difference from previous occasions was that the islanders themselves were now resigned to the inevitability of evacuation.

When the *Hebrides* paid her first visit of the season on 31 May it was found that the St Kildans had not made any attempt to sow crops or prepare for another winter. A dwindling, ageing population, too few now to carry on an independent existence, and all too aware of the far better conditions prevailing on the mainland, had many reasons for demanding evacuation. Not the least of these was their isolation, aggravated by the lack of mail after having been accustomed to a more frequent service for some years.

As late as July 1930, however, when talk of evacuation was in the air, the Post Office was still attempting to negotiate with the Fleetwood Fishing Vessel Owners' Association for a tentative winter service. At long last everyone realised that mail facilities for the island could not be regarded in terms of postal revenue and consequently a monthly winter service by trawler was envisaged, at a cost of £15 a trip, to be borne jointly by the Post Office and the Scottish Department of Health. Eight trawler companies at Aberdeen were approached but all refused to tender. An old standby in the past had been the Norwegian whalers, but the whaling station at Loch Bunaveneader was now closed. The Iago Steam Trawler Co. of Fleetwood alone appeared agreeable to carrying the mails – but by that time the St Kildans were preparing to abandon their island home.

Nine

The Evacuation
of St Kilda

On 29 May 1930 the *Hebrides* made her first visit of the season. The weather was perfect and the sun was setting when she sailed into Village Bay and gave a loud blast on her siren. One of her passengers was a young journalist named Iain Anderson who had long cherished an ambition to visit the loneliest of the British Isles. He subsequently filed a long report which appeared in *The Scotsman* of 6 June. He graphically described the eagerness of the islanders whose boat came out from the shore before the anchor was lowered, and scrambled aboard:

> Each poured forth a torrent of greeting. Question and answer were spoken in one breath. The high-pitched rapid Gaelic spoken by the islanders was remarkably contrasted when they lapsed into English, in which they spoke in a soft, musical intonation, as if caressing each word ere it left their lips.

Anderson was anxious to get ashore and was in the first boatload of passengers to be greeted by the pack of howling dogs at the jetty. This boat contained the sacks of mail, and he 'followed these to their distribution centre, which is not the actual post office of the village, but a roughly built wooden hut at the head of the jetty and within a stone's throw of the sea, the post office itself being, along with the houses, about a quarter of a mile back from the shore'. He interviewed several of the islanders and formed the impression that 'they are determined to leave the island, and that they will remain adamant on that point'. He also responded to four proposals made in *The Scotsman* by John Mathieson a few days earlier: that the lighthouse steamer should make regular calls in the eight winter months; that a tweed factory be established on the island to improve the quality of the cloth produced; that a granite quarry be created to provide steady employment; and that a meteorological station be erected, complete with an airstrip. All four were quite impracticable, partly because of the difficulties in landing on Hirta but mainly on account of the fact that St Kilda now had only eight able-bodied men, hardly sufficient to man the island's boats, let alone work in quarries or factories.

By the time the *Dunara Castle* made her visit to St Kilda on Friday 13 June, the die was cast. Norman MacKinnon, head of the island's largest family, had suffered more than most from the privations of the previous winter and had no intention of suffering another one like that. He had made up his mind to remove his family of nine to the mainland. The MacKinnons represented almost a quarter of the population and as a result of their decision the other islanders had little option but to follow suit. This achieved the result which Williamina Barclay had been striving for over the previous months. Contrary to a statement in an article of July 2005 in *The Scotsman* which described her as quiet-spoken and a member of the wealthy Glasgow shipbuilding family of Barclay, she was a native of Banchory, noted for her powerful north-eastern accent and eyes that fixed one with a piercing stare. She was a commanding figure and the sort of person that instinctively led others. By contrast, Dugald Munro, the last of the missionaries, was a rather meek and mild man who readily deferred to the nurse, especially in matters of such great importance. Her strident letters to the Home and Health Department had ended up on the desk of the Under-Secretary of State for Scotland, Tom Johnston, one of the ablest and probably most energetic of the Labour Government. Johnston was on board the *Dunara*, having decided to visit the island and assess the situation for himself. As a result, he took swift action, realising that if the islanders were not removed by the end of August they would have to endure yet another winter there. That this complex project was accomplished in little more than two months is testament to Johnston's energy and drive.

Nurse Barclay was also on board the *Dunara* on this voyage, returning from a spell of leave on the mainland. When interviewed by a reporter from the *Glasgow Herald* as she boarded the ship on 10 June, however, she was uncharacteristically reticent: 'She would express no view on the project [evacuation], remarking that her job was to attend to the health of the St Kildans. She was happy in her job, and would return to the island with the pleasurable anticipations of completing her full spell of duty.'

Tom Johnston was accompanied by T.B.W. Ramsay, MP for the Western Isles, who had the unique distinction of being the first member for that constituency to visit his St Kilda constituents. The Under-Secretary of State spent five hours ashore and interviewed each family in their own homes. This reinforced his view that the island should be evacuated, and the sooner the better.

In this he was at odds with Ramsay. 'I think it will be a great pity,' he said, 'if these people are taken off an island which has been their home for hundreds of years. With science advancing, such a move seems to be unnecessary.' He felt that the problem of St Kilda and the entire Hebrides 'should be met by the promotion of proper communications and increased facilities all over the islands for medical and surgical treatment'.

These comments reinforced the views of another passenger, the celebrated novelist and island enthusiast, Compton Mackenzie. His comments to a journalist from the *Daily Record* were even more pithy:

> I think the idea of evacuation is ridiculous. I am not convinced of the need for it. The majority of these people want to leave, but they don't know what they are doing. They have no real conception of what lies before them on the mainland, but seem to think only of some wonderful new world.

Compton, who lived for some time on the otherwise uninhabited Shiant Isles and later settled on Barra for many years, was dismissed as an incurable romantic, but his assessment of the situation was very shrewd and, sadly, all too prophetic regarding the disillusionment which set in once the St Kildans reached the mainland.

The *Daily Record* reporter mentioned that 'Someone also spoke of St Kilda being used as a point of tourist interest in the summer months, with an island staff on duty, during the holiday period', but Tom Johnston dismissed that notion out of hand. He and his companions had had a very stormy voyage and many of them, including Johnston himself, were prostrate with sea-sickness most of the time. Why anyone would wish to visit such a remote place in such hellish conditions was quite beyond his comprehension.

The forty-odd passengers on this excursion were already aware that the St Kildan community was coming to an end, judging by the rather poignant messages on the postcards they sent to friends and family. Somebody on this trip took a photograph of Annie Ferguson, Neil's wife, in the doorway of the post office, her hands filled with bundles of socks. The passengers crowding round the door are clad in sou'westers and mackintoshes, reflecting the dismal weather which prevailed that summer.

Tourists buying socks from Annie Ferguson (Neil's wife) at the post office door, July 1930. It appears to have been a typically wet summer day, judging by the mackintoshes and sou'westers worn by the visitors. The lady behind Mrs Ferguson clutches some postcards, destined to become much-prized mementoes.

When the *Hebrides* called in late July she had on board an official of the Scottish Department of Agriculture, accompanied by two shepherds from North Uist and one from Berneray with their trained dogs to round up the flock of Blackface sheep that grazed on Hirta. The celebrated native sheep were, at that time, confined to the island of Soay whence they derived their name, but they belonged to the MacLeod of MacLeod and remained unmolested. When the ship called again on 6 August 667 sheep were put aboard, destined for the livestock market in Oban. The remaining sheep, rather more than 500, were rounded up in the days immediately prior to the evacuation, and then ferried in batches of a dozen out to the *Dunara Castle* on her final visit that summer.

In mid-August the *Dunara* brought out the representatives of the Scottish Departments of Education, Health and Forestry, Messrs Henderson, McManus and Hosie, who found time from their manifold official duties to explore the island. There are several photographs of 'the men from the Ministry' posing against a cleit or inspecting the ancient underground dwelling known as the Fairy House, in their three-piece suits which included plus-fours, the customary garb of the male tourists of the period. They were joined by other bureaucrats, including Thomas W. Paterson of the Registrar General's Office, responsible for checking the registers of births, marriages and deaths. Paterson noted that no births had been recorded since early in 1928. Dr Alexander Shearer from the Home and Health Department and a Mr MacAulay from the Department of Agriculture were also in the party which spent over a week on the island.

Shearer and George Henderson had the ticklish task of sorting out who was to foot the bill for the evacuation. It was Dr Shearer who came up with the solution. He procured a quantity of sixpenny stamps from the little post office and persuaded the head of each household to sign his name across it, affixed to a declaration which effectively absolved the Home and Health Department. The St Kildans, in effect, promised to re-imburse the Department for 'such sums as may be incurred by them regarding the removal of family, goods and effects (other than sheep), temporary accommodation in the course of removal, the purchase of furniture and furnishings for the new houses and execution of minor repairs required, also sum paid by way of maintenance until wages due to the islanders has been paid'. The money owed by the St Kildans, however, was not to exceed the sum obtained from the sale of their sheep on the mainland.

At first the St Kildans were very reluctant to help round up the sheep. Why should they perform such an arduous task for nothing when they stood to gain nothing for their efforts? Eventually MacAulay agreed that the men should be paid £1 per day while this work was carried out. In total it cost the authorities upwards of £506 to transport 1,200 sheep, including the wages of the three shepherds and the charges for dipping and penning the animals at Oban prior to the sale on 3 September.

There was another sailing of the *Hebrides*, on 23 August and, on this occasion, the passengers included the Earl and Countess of Cassilis and the Duke and Duchess of Grafton. A sudden squall struck Village Bay just as this aristocratic party was approaching the little jetty and it was only the superb skill of the seamen that prevented the longboat being smashed on the rocks.

Sheep on the jetty, awaiting transportation to the cattle mart at Oban, August 1930. These were not the famous Soay sheep (at that time confined to the island whose name they bore), but a flock of mixed Cheviot and Blackface which had traditionally grazed on Hirta and Boreray.

Manhandling sheep into a rowing boat, August 1930. This was the age-old method of removing livestock from St Kilda, the prelude to an even rougher handling as the animals were slung aboard the steamer.

The Duke and Duchess of Grafton with the Earl and Countess of Cassilis, August 1930. Their aristocratic presence aboard the *Hebrides* roused the animosity of young Alasdair Alpin MacGregor.

The national press was now full of announcements about the impending evacuation of St Kilda. Messrs McCallum, Orme & Co. announced in *The Scotsman* on 19 and 20 August that the *Dunara Castle* would leave Greenock on Thursday 21 August. Alexander Ferguson did not travel out to St Kilda to witness the evacuation, but that morning he crossed the Clyde from his home at Old Kilpatrick to witness the departure of the old steamer from the Custom House Quay. There are press photographs showing a postman handing over the last mailbag for St Kilda to the purser, Mr Wylie; just over his shoulder can be seen a rather grim-faced 'AG'.

The latest hour of posting letters for St Kilda at the Head Post Office in Glasgow was 11.45 a.m. on the day of sailing and 10 a.m. from Edinburgh. Considering that postmark collecting was, in 1930, still embryonic, it is surprising to note the large amount of stamped addressed envelopes sent to St Kilda for despatch by Neil Ferguson with the last date of his postmark. The combined mails landed at St Kilda from the *Hebrides* on 23 August and the *Dunara Castle* four days later were the largest he ever handled. Most of the mail landed on 23 August consisted of stamped addressed envelopes and postcards sent under cover to the postmaster for despatch on the last out-going mail. Neil, assisted by Alasdair Alpin MacGregor, who was covering the evacuation as special correspondent for *The Times*, sorted the mail and postmarked it on 27 August for despatch on the *Dunara Castle*.

Tom Johnston, the Under-Secretary of State at the Scottish Office, had been at pains to insist that the evacuation of St Kilda should be conducted in a dignified manner and, as a result, there was a total embargo on journalists and press photographers – they would have a field day when the St Kildans reached the mainland. The sole exception was thirty-one-year-old Alasdair Alpin MacGregor, who may have wangled the trip on the *Hebrides* in his capacity as a minor civil servant in London (actually private secretary to the Chancellor of the Duchy of Lancaster, Sir Oswald Moseley). Landing on 23 August, he spent four days on St Kilda as a house guest of Neil Ferguson. Alasdair Alpin (as he liked to be called) had Lewis connections and had been raised in Easter Ross and Inverness, so he was just the man to cover the evacuation. As well as being duly appointed special correspondent for *The Times*, he also filed reports for the *Daily Express* and the *Quarterly Review*.

The articles he tapped out on his portable typewriter from the guestroom in the postmaster's house would later be expanded into a book of 316 pages entitled *A Last Voyage to St Kilda* (Cassell, 1931) in conscious emulation of the first book, published by Martin Martin in 1698, *A Late Voyage to St Kilda*. MacGregor was also a skilled photographer, and the many pictures in his book were augmented by photographs taken by A.M. Cockburn in 1927–28. MacGregor's book had a six-line sub-title which also seems to owe something to Martin Martin: 'Being the observations and adventures of an egotistical private secretary who was alleged to have been "warned off" that island by Admiralty officials when attempting to emulate Robinson Crusoe at the time of its Evacuation'. This verbose sub-title set the tone for the book as a whole.

Like George Seton back in the 1870s, MacGregor relied heavily on material in previously published books about the island, but this was more than offset by his own lively, often highly opinionated, comments and descriptions which revealed a great deal about the man himself. He would later build a considerable reputation for books about the Highlands and Islands viewed through rose-tinted spectacles, which led Compton Mackenzie to lampoon him, creating the fictional writer Hector Hamish Mackay when wishing to include a florid description in his comic novels. The sickly romanticising, often descending into bathos, that permeated MacGregor's writings came to a sudden halt with the publication of his book *The Western Isles* (Robert Hale, 1949), a savagely critical and grossly exaggerated account of the islands and their way of life. It was such a tendentious piece of work that the Lewis Association took the unprecedented

Alasdair Alpin MacGregor on the deck of the
Dunara Castle, August 1930. The private secretary
of Sir Oswald Moseley, he was the special
correspondent of *The Times* at the evacuation
of St Kilda and published a book about it the
following year. The kilt and tam-o'-shanter
bonnet would have immediately marked him
out to the St Kildans as a *towrie* (tourist).

step the following year of devoting the whole of their annual report to correcting
the factual errors and setting the record straight, concluding that a man who was
a self-professed atheist, vegetarian, anti-vivisectionist and teetotaller was not best
qualified to write a book about the red-blooded people of the Hebrides.

MacGregor was a poor example of the London Scot, living in Chelsea with his
sister Catriona. For most of his life he was a 'confirmed bachelor' but in the 1960s
he took to wife the widow of a naval officer who had a mellowing influence on
him to some extent before his death in 1970. We shall encounter him again in the
final chapter, but as a result of his efforts in 1930 we have a detailed account of
the final days of the St Kilda community. There is a certain breathlessness about
his narrative, written in the present tense. Although often unbearably prolix (140
pages pass before we get the first reference to St Kilda) his account provides us
with interesting asides, one of which describes his accommodation – 'a large cabin
containing the only bath aboard the *Hebrides*' – which he shared with 'a young and
intelligent Glasgow fellow named Iain Anderson'. It will be remembered that he
had visited St Kilda for the first time two months previously and filed some articles
for *The Scotsman*. On this trip he had no official accreditation but still managed to
send a feature to the newspaper. He would also contribute his fair share of highly
romanticised writing about the Highlands and Islands in the years ahead.

Early in MacGregor's narrative, the reader learned that the two men occupying the deck state-room were informed by James Adam, the chief steward, that they could only have it so long as they were prepared to vacate it as early as 6 a.m. if any other passenger insisted on having a bath. As luck would have it 'a certain earl and countess, as also Sir Tom Noddy, had indicated their intentions, independently, of having a bath at daybreak'. The intentions of the Earl and Countess of Cassilis, with the Duke of Grafton, were neatly scuppered by young Anderson who calmly informed the steward that the bathroom had been 'the retreat of a number of *hors-de-combat* passengers'. Thus 'the bathing propensities of the splashing nobility' were foiled. This provoked a long paragraph, ending: 'But just fancy members of the nobility of Scotland coming aboard a ship of this kind without having attended to their personal ablutions!' Such gems, however, were relatively few and far between amid the turgid prose. We learn that the wireless operator on the *Hebrides* at this time was Alasdair MacRae who, like MacGregor, played the bagpipes and sang Gaelic songs into the wee small hours throughout the voyage in the confines of the tiny stateroom: 'God! The skirl of the pipes goes to my head quicker than would the ruddiest wine, teetotaller though I be.'

MacGregor was a prominent campaigner against vivisection, the use of animals in laboratory experiments. He lost his dog, Torquil the Timid, in 1930, and thus may be forgiven for using a picture of this black collie for the frontispiece, as well as effusively dedicating the book to him, but on the subject of the St Kilda dogs he became positively incandescent. Unlike the urban dogs of London, the island collies were wild curs, the terror of many a timid tourist and utterly hopeless as sheepdogs. The wonder is that the island should have supported so many of them. When the St Kildans learned that mainland dogs required a licence costing 7s 6d a year it was decided communally to put them down. Dr Shearer, assisted by Surgeon Lieutenant-Commander Arnold Pomfret from HMS *Harebell*, did kill two of the dogs using hydrocyanic pellets in a hastily improvised gas chamber in one of the cottages, but this experiment with a prototype of Cyklon B was probably more hazardous to the operators than the animals. The St Kildans thereupon insisted in disposing of them in the traditional manner, tying large stones round their necks and throwing them off the end of the jetty to drown.

MacGregor was a dog-lover, of course, but he was also a practical man: 'Had I dreamed before leaving for this outpost that the Government scheme made no provision for those unfortunate creatures, I would have brought a humane killer with me.' He was also in touch with the National Canine Defence League, who had agreed to buy licences for all the dogs, but nothing came of it. He stated: 'It is a damnable scandal that, even in a country *calling* itself civilized, such brutalities

Passengers on *Dunara Castle* looking towards the shore, 27 August 1930. It is interesting to note the variety of dress which was thought suitable for such a perilous journey, even in high summer. Everyone except young James Dryden (in mackintosh, beside the rail) is wearing some kind of headgear. Note the Inverness cape and plus-fours of the gentleman beside the funnel.

are perpetrated daily with complete impunity and complacency. These creatures certainly did *not* meet a painless end.' When the *Hebrides* paid her last visit to St Kilda on 10 September, bringing out a shipload of tourists to gape at the 'desert island', they were revolted to find the dock inlet choked with the bloated carcasses of the drowned dogs.

Only about thirty tourists were aboard when the *Dunara Castle* arrived at 5 p.m. on 27 August. Even the weather played its part in the final act of the human drama. The island had been enveloped in thick mists and drizzle every day since the *Hebrides* called, and on this day the weather was worse than before. The *Dunara* had been expected on 26 August but had been delayed at Obbe because of severe gales. Village Bay was now like a millpond but the island was still surrounded by a thick fog that fateful day and the ship was almost on top of its destination before the island was visible. First of all the solitary rock called Levenish loomed up out of the mist and the passengers thought that this was Hirta itself, but another 2 miles steaming brought them abreast of Oiseval and they glided into the bay. Those on shore were alerted to the approaching ship by St Kilda radar – the excited barking of the island's half-wild dogs – and then there was something eerie about the elderly steamer emerging from the fog. MacGregor recorded the ship's arrival: 'About four in the afternoon, when the mists are at their densest, a small boy comes running in to assure us that he heard the steamer's whistle. More than an hour elapses before the ship is actually visible… Even from the quay only half of her masts can be seen for the fog that is in it.'

A fine profile of the *Dunara Castle* on a postcard of 1930 published by McCallum Orme and sold aboard the ship.

The back of the postcard bears the signatures of all the passengers on the evacuation voyage (plus Peter Ferguson, the wireless officer). From the scrapbook compiled by James Dryden.

The tide was ebbing and another hour passed before the St Kilda boats could be launched. Because of the state of the tide the *Dunara* would be delayed at St Kilda for at least eight hours. In fact it took several hours to ferry the sheep, in batches of twelve, followed by the cattle. Four calves were transferred by boat but the cows were towed out with ropes around their necks.

Considering the tremendous interest in the evacuation of St Kilda it is surprising that the *Dunara Castle* only carried about thirty passengers on this final voyage. They included a giant Dutchman in kilt and tam-o'-shanter bonnet – Baron Willem Mackay van Ophemert, otherwise known as the Master of Reay. Several years later he succeeded his cousin as chief of the Clan Mackay and, on taking the title Lord Reay, became naturalised. He wished to remain on the island after it was evacuated, hoping to spend a week or two in total solitude before the *Hebrides* called in September with the last excursion of the year. To this end he had provided himself with ample supplies of food as well as a sleeping bag, but he was compelled to re-board the *Dunara* the following morning by the commander of the *Harebell* which took the islanders to the mainland. Baron Mackay had to be content with posting the very last letter in the post office mailbox, addressed to his good friend George Brumell of Bournemouth, the doyen of British postmark collectors at that period.

The eager passengers scrambled ashore and made a beeline for the post office to buy postcards and get the coveted 'last day' postmark. While Neil Ferguson was preoccupied with packing his worldly goods and transporting them down to the jetty, MacGregor stood in for him as postmaster. As the evening cleared, the thirty tourists came ashore and besieged the tiny post office. Most of them were already armed with postcards purchased on board the *Dunara*, 'but I succeed in getting off on them another two or three hundred, together with requisite stamps'. Before the evening was over the stock of penny stamps ran out, 'But today I have acquired such excellent salesmanship that I am able to persuade the tourists that the occasion justifies their placing three-halfpenny stamps on the postcards they are now purchasing. Numbers of them ask for halfpenny stamps, and are disappointed that our supplies do not permit them adding to the postmaster's labours in this respect. Halfpenny stamps are in demand among those who are desirous that their communications should bear at least two stamp marks.'

Though each passenger had paid £10 for the trip, 'the more officious of them have kicked up hell with Ferguson at the post-office when he has run out of penny stamps, and have flatly refused to pay the extra halfpenny on the plea that the post-office is a Government institution, and ought to be conducted as such'. This explains why some of the cards date-stamped 27 August and all of those date-stamped 28 August bear penny-halfpenny stamps.

The most difficult and potentially hazardous operation involved the manhandling of the island cows on to the *Dunara Castle*. The terrified animal has a rope tangled round its horns to assist loading by the ship's crew.

A St Kilda cow tethered on the deck of the *Dunara Castle*, below one of the ship's lifeboats.

One of the Uist shepherds helping to round up the sheep brought in a parcel just after 2 a.m. the following morning. Conscientiously MacGregor changed the date slug after midnight and consequently a few items are known with the true last date of 28 August. Due to his lack of experience, MacGregor accidentally reversed the order of the day and month slugs so that the date read AU 28 instead of vice versa. The *Dunara Castle* had taken away the many sacks of mail postmarked 27 August when it departed at noon the following day.

Shortly after dawn on 28 August the *Dunara* blew her whistle to rouse the exhausted islanders after only a couple of hours' sleep. The rest of the livestock was soon ferried out and stowed away. The sun rose to a warm day, the thick mists rapidly rising off the steep hillsides. The sea remained calm – a perfect day for the evacuation. Soon after 7 a.m. a speck appeared on the horizon. It materialised as HMS *Harebell*, the fishery protection cruiser which had been entrusted with the removal of the St Kildans themselves.

The previous evening a strange ship, painted grey-blue, had entered the bay and the St Kildans imagined that this was the *Harebell*. But she had the French tricolour at her stern and the sailors who came ashore in a jolly-boat had pom-poms on their hats. The ship turned out to be the French cruiser *Ancre*, on a goodwill cruise of the British Isles. She had been in Stornoway some days previously and there encountered the *Harebell* and learned of the impending evacuation of St Kilda. Now she had come south to Hirta out of curiosity. Macgregor described the occasion: 'A happy band of Froggies comes ashore… Many of them, clad in white tunics, spend the afternoon in climbing Conachair and the Mullach Mòr, and in rolling huge stones and boulders down the hillsides and valleys.' The ship spent the night in the bay and tarried the following day but left soon after the arrival of the *Harebell*.

Tourists milling round the post office for the last day postmark. The men in their cloth caps and ladies in cloche hats (earnestly scribbling their postcards) contrast with the homespuns of the island girls on the right, chatting to their fellow St Kildan, Peter Ferguson (in naval cap). Note the bale of hand-woven tweed in the foreground.

The arrival of the fishery protection cruiser HMS *Harebell* on the afternoon of 28 August 1930. She is shown rounding the island of Dùn to enter Village Bay.

French sailors at the jetty, with the cruiser *Ancre* in background. This ship from Cherbourg was on a courtesy cruise round the Western Isles when she heard of the impending evacuation, and arrived in time to witness the last day of the St Kildans, although the matelots seem to have amused themselves ashore mainly by rolling boulders down the steep hillsides.

HMS *Harebell* in dock at Birkenhead, her home port. By the 1930s she was the senior vessel in the Fishery Protection Squadron.

The *Dunara Castle*, her decks laden with piles of spinning wheels and other furniture, weighed anchor at noon and set sail for Oban – a voyage of seventeen hours – with MacGregor, Baron Mackay and the other tourists on board. The St Kildans themselves would follow shortly by courtesy of the Royal Navy. HMS *Harebell* was a Flower Class sloop, commissioned on 10 May 1918 (five days before St Kilda's brief encounter with the German submarine) and scrapped shortly before the outbreak of the Second World War in 1939. She never heard a shot fired in action. She had a gross tonnage of 1,250 and a top speed of 16 knots. Her main armament consisted of two 4.7in guns mounted aft and a pair of 3-pounder anti-aircraft guns. She was one of a very large class of sloops, constructed from the outbreak of the First World War onwards for escort, minesweeping and general duties. While many of this class were scrapped or sold off in 1919–20 *Harebell* was retained as a fishery protection cruiser, based at Birkenhead, where many of her crew had their wives and families. She was, by 1930, the senior ship of the Fishery Protection Squadron.

Above: The cutter from HMS *Harebell*, with the islanders' belongings, towing a longboat similarly laden, on the evening of 28 August 1930.

Right: Sailors hauling an islander's chest aboard the *Harebell* on the evening before the evacuation of St Kilda.

Below: Cutter and jolly-boat leaving the *Harebell* for the jetty to pick up further islanders' chattels. The cutter appears to be a motor-boat with a sturdy superstructure, ideal for operations in the rough weather of the North Atlantic.

A petty officer in one of the ship's boats, supervising the loading of the St Kildans' possessions aboard the *Harebell*, 28 August 1930.

At the time of her historic mission her skipper was Commander Barrow who had to exercise all his diplomatic skills in handling the St Kildans, who were irked that the Navy arrived only after all the heavy work had been done. He was anxious to be off as soon as possible, but there was much murmuring in the village that they would not be hustled on the last day 'if the entire Navy should come out for them'. The *Dunara Castle* had already departed before the *Harebell* weighed anchor so there was no MacGregor around to chronicle the last moments.

According to the Government officials who remained to the bitter end and accompanied the islanders on the *Harebell*, the St Kildans refused the help of the sailors to carry their personal belongings down to the jetty, but the Navy men spent the afternoon ferrying chests, trunks and assorted bundles out to the ship. A few of the sailors took the opportunity to mail some of the remaining postcards (published by Alexander Ferguson). Commander Pomfret complained at having to affix threehalfpenny stamps. The French sailors had the last laugh: threehalfpence was the foreign postcard rate at the time.

HMS *Harebell* had been on a routine tour round the Scottish islands when she was ordered to evacuate the St Kildans. From Stornoway she steamed south to Oban to pick up some other Government officials and then left that port at 6 p.m. on Wednesday 27 August. By 10 p.m. she had passed Rudha nan Gall on the northern tip of Mull and headed into the Minch in thick fog. She sailed round Barra Head at 2 a.m. and sighted St Kilda at 5.45 a.m. At 7.23 a.m. precisely, her engines stopped and she dropped anchor in Village Bay. All boats were lowered at

8 a.m. and parties went ashore soon afterwards. This task proceeded all morning, the sailors returning to the ship at noon for their mid-day meal. With a full tide at 1 p.m. *Harebell* weighed anchor and shifted berth inshore to make it easier for all hands embarking the islanders' belongings. The sea remained dead flat calm all afternoon and the sailors sweltered in the unseasonably hot sunshine. By 9 p.m. the task was completed and the working parties returned to the ship.

The St Kildans spent a last night in their cottages. The ship's log laconically noted that at 5 a.m. on 29 August the second whaler was lowered: 'Embarked the inhabitants of St Kilda, 14 women, 13 men, 15 children.' The next entry was: 'Everyone on board. Hoisted boats. 0802 hrs Weighed. Proceeded 11.5 knots.' The weather was calm, the barometric pressure 1017 and the air temperature 57 degrees. A more detailed report was later sent to the Admiralty by Surgeon Lieutenant-Commander (later Rear Admiral) Pomfret: 'At 07.00 hours all the houses were locked and the people taken on board. Shortly afterwards they were looking their last at St Kilda as the *Harebell*, quickly increasing speed, left the island a blur on the horizon. Contrary to expectations they had been very cheerful throughout, though obviously very tired…'

The police sergeant from Lochmaddy, North Uist (within whose jurisdiction St Kilda lay), with Peter Ferguson (the *Dunara* wireless officer) and girls outside the post office, August 1930. Judging by their dress and hairstyle, the young ladies were tourists.

St Kildans on the *Princess Louise* on their way to Morvern. They are crowding on the bridge for a first glimpse of their new home on a remote part of the Scottish mainland. The man in the trilby hat beside the funnel was George Henderson from the Scottish Home and Health Department, who helped to superintend the evacuation.

The islanders were up very early, dressed in their Sabbath best. After morning prayers they placed an open Bible and a handful of meal on the table in each cottage, the peat fires were banked up and the doors closed but not locked, for none of them possessed such a security device. Then the St Kildans trudged along their little street and across the meadow to the jetty. The islanders took only clothing and small belongings – furniture and even crockery was left behind. Perhaps there was a feeling that if things did not work out for them on the mainland they would soon return and pick up their old way of life again.

The sea remained calm for the voyage to the mainland. On board ship the St Kildans were fed simply but substantially on bread and butter, mugs of tea and generous helpings of sliced beef and salmon with tinned meat and veg. The Admiralty subsequently sent a bill for £2 2s 6d to the Scottish Office for victualling the St Kildans. George Henderson sent a telegram to Tom Johnston, spending the weekend at his home in Kirkintilloch: 'Evacuation successfully carried out this morning.'

By 2 p.m. the ship had rounded Barra Head and three hours later passed Ardnamurchan, most westerly point on the mainland. At 6.37 a.m. the ship anchored in the Sound of Mull where twenty-four St Kildans were transferred to the small steamer *Princess Louise* for the last leg of their journey. It was only at this point that the enormity of what was happening engulfed the St Kildans. As Commander Pomfret noted: 'with the first actual separation came the first signs of emotion and men, women and children wept unrestrainedly as the last farewells were said.' The two dozen islanders were conveyed to Lochaline in Morvern, Argyll, where most of them would soon be settled in crofts strung out over several miles of wild moorland. On St Kilda the houses had stood cheek by

St Kildans going up the gangplank from the SS *Princess Louise* at Lochaline on the evening of 29 August 1930. The small boy, Norman Gillies, at the stern celebrated his eightieth birthday by revisiting St Kilda in August 2005, the seventy-fifth anniversary of the evacuation.

jowl, reinforcing the solidarity of the little community; in Morvern the people felt isolated and cut off, their sense of identity eroded. At Lochaline they were met by a large crowd of journalists and several cars – the first they had ever seen – which were on hand to convey them the last few miles to their new crofts. Their furniture, however, was taken off the *Princess Louise* and travelled by open boats to Ardness where it was manhandled over the rocks, rather like the stores were landed at St Kilda before the jetty was built.

The remaining St Kildans, along with the nurse, the missionary and his family, and assorted civil servants, left the *Harebell* at Oban shortly before 10 p.m. It had been a long and tiring day for them, but there was no rest, for the exhausted and bewildered migrants were immediately besieged by a gaggle of journalists and press photographers before they could be whisked off in a fleet of cars to their new homes. Initially Finlay MacQueen and the Fergusons were sent to Ardnarff, one of the most remote and least accessible spots in Wester Ross. A very poignant letter of 24 October 1930 by old Finlay, sent to John T. Mackenzie at Dunvegan, revealed the cruel insensitivity of officialdom (in the form of George Henderson) which had dumped the poor old man in the middle of nowhere and had even docked his old age pension to pay for his accommodation, leaving him penniless. A letter from Tom Johnston, dated 18 October (in reply to one from Finlay of 23 September stating how unhappy he was in his new surroundings) intimated that it was hoped soon to move him with the Ferguson family to Tulliallan in Fife where several St Kildans were offered employment with the Forestry Commission. For people who had spent their lives on an island without trees, that must have been a very strange experience.

The sale of the 1,200 sheep, ten cows and four calves took place at Oban on 3 September. Present at the sale was Tom Johnston, photographed afterwards commiserating with some of the St Kilda women. No wonder: the auction netted a mere £799 which barely covered the costs of removing them from St Kilda. The paltry sum left after the deduction of costs was a bitter disappointment to the St Kildans, but the result was as much as could have been expected in view of the poor condition of the beasts. Indeed, about a hundred sheep died soon after their arrival on the mainland. Months passed before the St Kildans received their miserable share of the proceeds. By contrast, the 1931 Honours List recorded the award of the decoration Commander of the Most Excellent Order of the British Empire (CBE) to Williamina Barclay for services to the St Kilda community.

The *Harebell* also carried the very last mail from St Kilda. Neil Ferguson dropped off the mailbag at the head post office in Oban, together with the date stamp and the mailbag seal. It is alleged that the brass seal was offered to Neil Ferguson as a memento of his postmastership but, with true Celtic lack of sentimentality, he declined the offer. On his arrival, Neil granted an interview to the editor of the *Oban Times*, A.E. Cameron, who obtained examples of the postmark dated 29 August 'by favour' on a parcel label and a postcard. In so doing, Ferguson reset the position of the day and month which MacGregor had muddled.

Apparently the date stamp and its type-box were sent on from Oban to Lochmaddy, to whose head post office St Kilda was subordinate. Contrary to normal practice, they were not forwarded to Edinburgh for ultimate disposal but held at Lochmaddy as interesting souvenirs. After many years they were sent to Edinburgh where they were retained at the General Post Office as curiosities. In 1957, when St Kilda was repopulated by the Royal Air Force, the date stamp was refurbished and sent to Lochmaddy to postmark mail coming off the island. It was employed for that purpose successively at Lochboisdale and Stranraer, whither St Kilda mails were routed by landing craft, but taken out of service in September 1958 and consigned, with other security scrap, to the bottom of the Bay of Biscay.

'Finis' was written to the St Kilda story with the instructions given in the *Post Office Circular* of 10 September 1930 which stated: 'The St Kilda Post Office was closed on 29th August, the date of the evacuation of the island. Official records should be amended where necessary. Any letters or parcels which may come to hand for St Kilda should circulate as for Oban, where arrangements have been made for their redirection to the addressees.'

A list of names of the St Kildans and their new addresses was held at Oban head post office to enable the redirection of mail. In spite of this, the occasional stray letter addressed to an erstwhile inhabitant continued to turn up as late as 1960.

Ten

Desert Island Days

Five families, numbering twenty-seven persons, were settled in the scattered crafting townships of Larachbeg, Ardness, Ardtornish, Achabeg, and Savary in the Morvern peninsula. It was one of the bleakest and most barren tracts of land in Scotland, fit only for afforestation, and thus the planting and tending of seedlings and saplings was entrusted to a people who had never seen a tree. Neil Ferguson was offered a position as sub-postmaster at Manish on the south-east coast of Harris but turned it down. In the end, he and his family, with old Finlay MacQueen, were moved from Ardnarff to Tulliallan near Culross in Fife, another of the Forestry Commission's projects. One of the Macdonalds, who had never seen paving other than the rude street on Hirta, was taken on by Ross-shire County Council as a road-mender.

With such strange surroundings and occupations, forced to make ends meet with regular, if small, wages, and cut off from the charity which had so often baled them out in the past, the St Kildans were homesick and heartsick. It is hardly surprising that they soon longed to return to their remote sea-girt isle and petitioned for resettlement there; but the Government had spent more than £1,200 removing them and was not inclined to waste money in sending them back whence they had come.

In 1931 McCallum Orme decided to cash in on the heightened interest in St Kilda as a result of its abandonment to the seabirds. The sailing programme followed the same pattern as in the years immediately preceding the evacuation but now the steamship company focused on the allure of St Kilda, with a new slogan: 'the Island that wants to be visited.' The *Hebrides* was scheduled to make four excursions, leaving Glasgow on 25 May, 15 June, 16 July and 17 August, while the *Dunara Castle* sailed on 18 June, 9 July and 10 August. That summer alone, almost 700 passengers booked on the St Kilda cruises.

In connection with the sailings scheduled for that summer, McCallum Orme approached the Post Office about reopening the sub-post office on St Kilda on a seasonal basis. A dozen St Kildans were allegedly returning for the summer and Neil Ferguson was said to have agreed to officiate as postmaster again. On making enquiries, however, the Post Office discovered that Neil Ferguson had been granted two months' leave of absence from the Forestry Commission to return to St Kilda for the express purpose of recovering some of his personal effects. No other St Kildans had applied for leave. When pressed for details, McCallum Orme said that the other eleven were all St Kildans who had left the island before 1930. The Post Office was sceptical and felt that the whole venture had been engineered by the shipping company for the purpose of promoting their tours. As the islanders' boats had been left behind, assistance by the St Kildans was necessary if the tourists were to land.

Sir Reginald MacLeod, who was still the proprietor at this time, strenuously opposed resettlement, even on a temporary basis, because of potential danger to the island's unique wildlife. The Post Office, in line with official Government policy, not only refused to reopen the post office but also to hand over to the steamship company any mail for St Kilda unless specifically addressed to the company's care.

One of the returning St Kildans that summer was Alexander Ferguson. When he heard that the Post Office refused to reopen the sub-office he procured a rectangular rubber date stamp to cachet the postcards which the tourists would be buying. His brother Neil 'reopened' the post office (i.e. opened up the tin shack adjoining his cottage) and did a brisk trade in Alexander's picture postcards to which he duly applied the St Kilda date stamp at the side. Neil came armed with a substantial stock of stamps which were affixed to the outgoing cards and duly cancelled at the first port of call on the homeward trip. The Ferguson date stamp has been recorded for every year up to and including 1939, normally struck in violet but sometimes in black ink, in conjunction with the postmarks of Lochmaddy, Lochboisdale, Harris, Uig, Dunvegan, Oban or even Greenock, depending on the route taken. The earliest date of use so far recorded is 12 July 1931, on mail taken off by the *Dunara Castle* during her second cruise of the season.

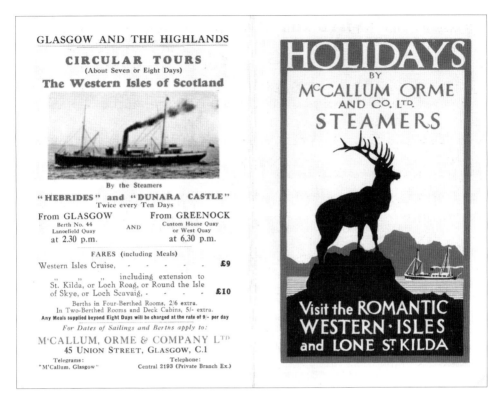

The McCallum Orme brochure of 1931, showing one of the company's steamers with the island of Dùn in the background. The stag motif on the cover was taking artistic licence to the extreme limit for there was never a deer within 50 miles of St Kilda.

The first cruise by the *Hebrides* left Glasgow on 25 May 1931 and reached St Kilda four days later. She was delayed owing to bad weather and was then forced by severe storms to beat a hasty retreat to Loch Eport in North Uist. The exiles, who were taking wool to weave on the looms they had left behind, were very disappointed. They tried to land again two days later and were again forced back by exceptionally low tides and a heavy swell. When they did eventually land on 19 June they discovered that the houses had been looted of their remaining contents and damage done to doors, windows and roofs by visiting trawlermen who had not been long in taking advantage of the islanders' evacuation to salvage what little there was of value left behind. As a result, Sir Reginald MacLeod officially appointed Neil Gillies as 'watcher' on St Kilda, a post which he held every summer until August 1939. News of the looting was communicated to the newspapers by ship's radio via Malin Head and appeared in the national dailies on 24 June.

GLASGOW & WEST HIGHLANDS

S.S. " HEBRIDES "

S.S. " DUNARA CASTLE "

For Dates of Sailings and Berths apply to :

M'CALLUM, ORME & COMPANY L™.

45 UNION STREET, GLASGOW, C.1

Telegrams :	Telephone :
" M'Callum, Glasgow "	Central 7126 (Private Branch Ex.)

The back of this brochure shows the *Hebrides* passing Duart Castle (top) and the *Dunara Castle* off Rodel at the entrance to the Sound of Harris (bottom), with the company emblem in the centre.

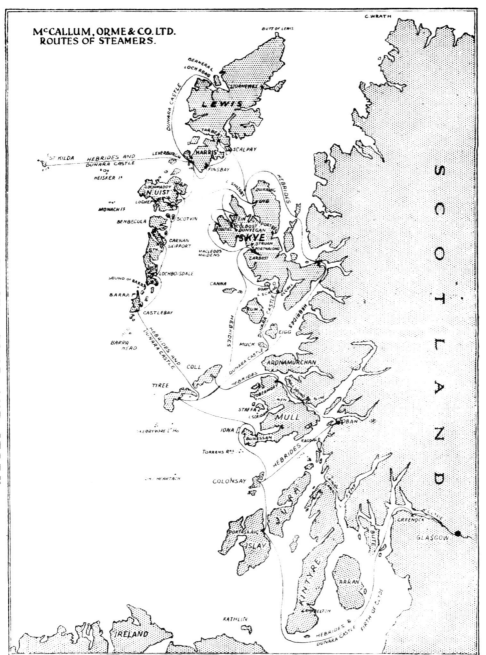

Map in the 1931 brochure showing the routes taken by McCallum Orme's steamers to the 'isles of sunset, song and story', neatly summing up the romanticism of remote places like St Kilda, far removed from grim reality.

The cabin plan for the *Dunara Castle* reveals the cramped and spartan conditions of the sleeping quarters.

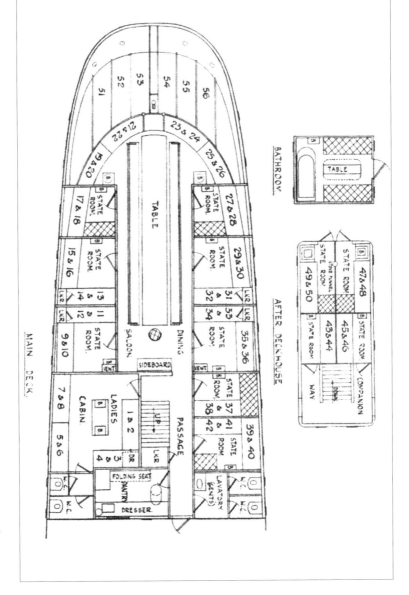

The cabin plan for the *Hebrides* shows that the accommodation on the sister ship was very similar, though the ships had been designed and constructed by different companies. The chief difference appears to have been the bathroom with twin bunks (upper right) – the 'stateroom' occupied by MacGregor and Iain Anderson.

McCallum Orme also reproduced their first brochure cover on a 'poster stamp', shown here on the back of an envelope from St Kilda with the Ferguson rubber date stamp (first day of use – 20 July 1931).

A McCallum Orme postcard of the early 1930s depicting the SS *Hebrides*. Examples of these cards bearing the Ferguson date stamp and occasionally the ships' cachets, with postmarks of the places where they were eventually posted, are very much sought after by collectors.

Alexander Ferguson (described in the newspapers as 'Acting Prime Minister of St Kilda') reported that the culprits were believed to be the crew of a Belgian trawler which was observed by some British trawlers. The *Daily Express* made some mistake surely in its report that, as the landing on Boreray was much easier than on Hirta, there was a fear that foreign trawlers would land on that island and slaughter the 300 Cheviot sheep which had been left there. 'AG' mysteriously hinted at clues left by the thieves and this may have been an allusion to graffiti in French scrawled on one of the interior walls of the church. The returning islanders were outraged and devastated at the wanton destruction – doors kicked down and windows smashed – apart from the theft of spinning wheels and fishing gear. Neil Gillies, writing to James Dryden (an Edinburgh stamp dealer) on 12 July, told him that he had managed to send off a St Kilda mailboat, adding: 'them Belgians that broke in on the houses took all the buoys away except one or two so I do hope that you will receive it safe.' The mailboat, with sheepskin buoy attached, was recovered at Grimsay and its contents forwarded to Dryden but the mailboat itself appears to have been retained by the finder.

These newspaper reports prompted a descent on St Kilda on 25 July by the fishery cruiser *Norna*, one of whose crew posted a card at St Kilda that day reporting that the ship had come upon four French luggers but that they did not have their nets down and therefore escaped arrest for illegal fishing.

In the summer of 1931 a party of undergraduates from the universities of Oxford and Cambridge descended on St Kilda. Each had a specific scientific interest to be applied to the study of an island that had so recently lost its human population. The St Kilda house mouse (*Mus musculus muralis*), so dependent on its human hosts, was dying out. Only about a dozen specimens were trapped. A year later they were believed to be extinct. Their sturdier cousin, the St Kilda fieldmouse (*Apodemus sylvaticus hirtensis*) had moved in on the cottages and outbuildings. The twelve young men included John Buchan, son and heir of the famous novelist and Canadian governor-general, Lord Tweedsmuir. Another was Tom Harrisson who later became the pioneer of mass observation and spent most of his life in Sarawak and other parts of South-East Asia. The budding ornithologists, zoologists, entomologists and anthropologists combined their reports in *St Kilda Papers, 1931*, never publicly released, although twenty-five copies were deposited in various national and university libraries some years later. The preface sourly noted: 'The whole ecological experiment has already been damaged by allowing the islanders to go back each summer since the evacuation.'

Sir Reginald MacLeod of MacLeod received hundreds of letters from every part of Britain, and even some from abroad, from people who were anxious to get 'away from it all' and settle on St Kilda, but he either refused or omitted to respond. Relieved at last of a human burden which latterly had been a drain on the MacLeod resources, he was now looking around for a purchaser. In September 1931 he sold the St Kilda archipelago to the Earl of Dumfries (later fifth Marquess of Bute). The sum was £3,000 – exactly what Norman MacLeod of MacLeod had paid to Sir John Macpherson MacLeod sixty years earlier. The Earl, a keen ornithologist, wished to preserve St Kilda as a bird sanctuary for himself and his friends, fellow naturalists. It was following his purchase that some of the aboriginal sheep were brought over from neighbouring Soay in June 1934 and are one of the principal features of Hirta to this day. The Earl and his party were conveyed thither aboard the *Dunara Castle* whose purser sent a telegram to the *Glasgow Herald* on 11 June so that readers of that newspaper might be kept up to date.

The new proprietor had the manse, renamed 'House of Oiseval', refurbished, including the installation of a bathroom complete with running water, for his family and guests, while visiting naturalists were also accommodated in the factor's house. The St Kildans themselves were given the opportunity to return for brief periods in the summer months, several of them, such as Neil Gillies and David Macdonald, even finding temporary employment as his lordship's caretakers and coast-watchers. Thereafter Lord Dumfries visited St Kilda each summer.

In 1932 the *Hebrides* called at the island on 22 June, 21 July, 15 August and 20 August; exact details for the *Dunara Castle* have not been recorded but she is known to have called at St Kilda on three occasions in the same period. George Blair, the purser on board the *Hebrides*, always made a point of sending a telegram to the *Glasgow Herald* which dutifully published a paragraph or two, even if only to comment on the weather. His opposite number on the *Dunara*, however, seldom bothered with such niceties.

It is not known whether the Earl ever visited St Kilda 'under his own steam', but by 1934 he was making use of the *Dunara Castle*. His 'house guests' on Hirta that summer included the naturalist Niall Rankin and his wife Lady Jean, as well as the Earl's mother, the Marchioness of Bute. A devout Catholic, the Earl also had his personal chaplain, Father J.M. McWilliam from Bellahouston, Glasgow, for spiritual comfort. A group photograph, showing the bearded Earl wearing a tam-o'-shanter bonnet, and the Rankins armed with shotguns, has Alexander Gillies Ferguson seated between the Countess and the Marchioness. On the

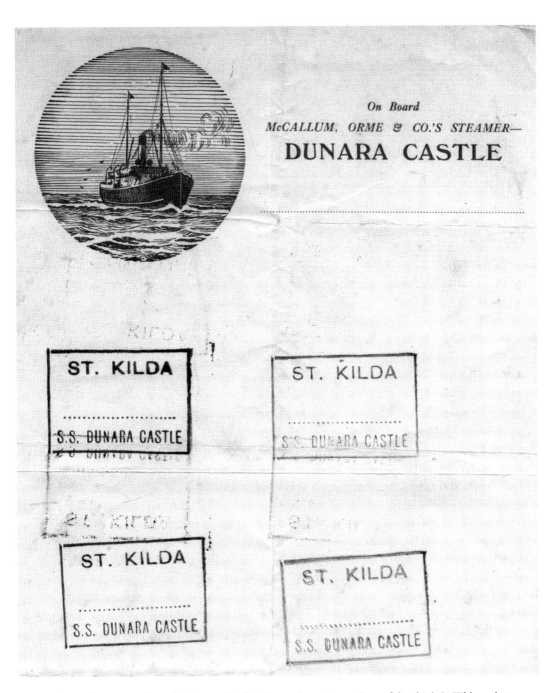

A sheet of notepaper from the *Dunara Castle* with specimen impressions of the ship's St Kilda cachet. So far, only a single example of this rubber stamp has been recorded on a postcard mailed from the island in the post-evacuation period.

Although the Earl of Dumfries (later Marquess of Bute) purchased St Kilda in order to preserve its unique ecology, he was not averse to using it for hunting parties. This photograph is from the summer of 1934 and shows the Earl and Countess with their guests and servants. Left to right (back row): Lady Jean Rankin and Colonel Sir Neil Rankin (with shotguns), the Earl (bearded and wearing a tam-o'-shanter) and Countess of Dumfries, Alexander Gillies Ferguson, the Marchioness of Bute and Father J. McWilliam, the Earl's chaplain; (front row): Neil Gillies (in Homburg hat), Sandy, the Earl's cook, and Malcolm Macdonald (who worked at the Savoy Hotel). Neil and Malcolm were St Kildans employed by the Earl as coast-watchers.

ground in front of them sit Neil Gillies (in a black Homburg hat), Sandy the cook (surname unknown), and Malcolm MacDonald, presumably the Earl's personal servant, for he later worked for many years in the Grosvenor House Hotel in London. In the author's possession is an envelope with a two-line cachet – 'HIRTA / ST. KILDA' – addressed to Father McWilliam in Glasgow, the postage stamp cancelled at Fleetwood on 28 July 1936, indicating that mail was still taken off the island by the trawlers and augmented the arrangements with the tourist steamers.

One of the visitors to St Kilda on the *Hebrides* in the summer of 1934 was C.L.D. Duckworth, co-author of the standard work *West Highland Steamers*, who mailed an envelope to himself bearing the Ferguson date stamp of 21 August, which was postmarked at Lochmaddy the following day.

The main beneficiary of the evacuation was the shipping company, for McCallum Orme now capitalised on 'Lone St Kilda'. Henceforward the island was an even greater attraction than ever and the cruises by the *Hebrides* and *Dunara Castle* were invariably fully booked. The company produced a new brochure with a tasteful cover in black and red showing a steamship with the craggy profile of Dùn in the background, though there was an excess of artistic licence in superimposing this with the silhouette of a stag at bay. Amazingly, the cost of the seven- or eight-day round trip remained at £10, with the same rates for superior cabins as before. The company even produced a label which had the same device as the cover, and this has been recorded on a handful of envelopes posted by returning St Kildans in 1931.

The text of the brochure was based on those previously published by the separate companies, the section headed 'The St Kilda Tour' being confined to two short paragraphs:

> From Lochmaddy two exciting and interesting hours pass as we sail through the Sound of Harris, passing Leverburgh on the Harris shore, the almost derelict town whose prosperity died with its founder – Lord Leverhulme. Ere morning is noon we reach St Kilda and its crescent shaped rugged bay, now uninhabited during winter – for the elements won the struggle for supremacy. In the Island bay we see the village a straggling line of grey stone cottages across this vast mountain amphitheatre, awesome in its cliffs, solitude, and wheeling, screaming seafowl.
>
> We walk along the deserted village path... But then you must see it for yourself. Already numerous books have been written about it. What can I tell here?

A second edition had a similar 'stag' motif but with greater use of eye-catching colour. By 1936 an even more ambitious twenty-page booklet was produced with a full-colour cover by J. Stanger showing the *Hebrides* with its red and black funnel, steaming up the Sound of Mull past Duart Castle. This revealed that the average sailing time from the Sound of Harris to St Kilda by either ship was five hours, but the *Hebrides* took seven hours on the return voyage to Tarbert (Harris) whereas the *Dunara Castle* took six hours on the voyage to Lochmaddy. An attractive feature of this booklet was the double spread of eight views of St Kilda. These brochures were complemented by handbills giving the actual timetable of sailings in general and the special cruises to St Kilda, Loch Roag, round Skye and Loch Scavaig in particular.

Front cover of the full-colour brochure, produced about 1934. The painting by J. Stanger shows one of the McCallum Orme steamers in the Sound of Mull, passing the ruins of Duart Castle.

In 1935 McCallum Orme's steamers chalked up nine trips between them. An echo of the Coronation ceremony of 1911 was the stunt that summer whereby some of the St Kildans returned to the island to weave a length of tweed to present to King George V as a Silver Jubilee present. That appears to have been the peak of the post-evacuation excursions, with ten trips by the two steamers between 25 May and 22 August. In 1936 the *Dunara* called on 4 and 24 June and 28 August, while the *Hebrides* was at St Kilda on 10 June and 27 July, the last of these being delayed by severe storms for several days. In 1937 the *Hebrides* called on 4 June, 1 and 22 July and 11 August. On 2 April that year the *Glasgow Herald* gave prominence to a statement by the Earl of Dumfries that he hoped that St Kilda might be repopulated. This led to a debate in the House of Commons on 7 May which concluded that there was no demand for facilities for the return of the former islanders. By that time most of the older inhabitants were dead.

Before the coastal steamers resumed their summer sailings St Kilda had an unexpected visitor at the end of May. In connection with the Coronation celebrations, the Corporation of the City of Glasgow organised a four-day cruise to the Western Isles aboard the *Tuscania II* of the Anchor Line. She carried 600 children who had been successful in the ballot for tickets, and fifty teachers. The ship cruised round the Inner and Outer Hebrides but the highlight of the trip was the visit to St Kilda. No landing took place, but the liner sailed round the archipelago before returning to the mainland. This liner of 16,900 tons was built at Fairfield, Govan, in 1919–21 and made her maiden voyage from Glasgow to New York, via Moville, Ireland, in September 1921. She was mainly used by the Anchor Line to take immigrants to America. For a time she was chartered to the Cunard Line on their Southampton–New York run, but in 1931 she returned to Glasgow and was laid up there until 1938 due to the Depression, so the Coronation cruise to St Kilda in 1937 was a welcome diversion. In 1939 she was sold to the Greek Line and renamed *Nea Hellas* (New Greece). She was used as a troopship during the Second World War but from 1946 to 1959 she worked the route from Piraeus to New York. She was then laid up and ultimately scrapped in Japan in 1961.

When the *Dunara Castle* called on 12 June 1937, the returning islanders were shocked to find that their cottages had been broken into again during the winter. Doubtless trawlermen were to blame, but by now there was precious little that was worth looting. The big St Kilda story that year concerned two young men who, according to the *Glasgow Herald*, were 'marooned' there. They were in fact Neil Gillies, styled by the newspaper as 'the representative of the Earl of Dumfries', and his cousin Alastair Ferguson (AG's son) who had been looking after the island all summer. They planned to leave St Kilda on the last trip of the *Dunara* on Tuesday 24 August but when the steamer called that day adverse weather conditions prevented the ship from entering the bay. This atrocious weather continued for several days and the ship returned to the Western Isles without effecting a landing.

McCallum Orme announced that they would divert the *Hebrides* the following week when she was on her regular run to Tarbert, Harris. With little improvement in the weather it seemed as if the *Hebrides* would not be able to make the dash from the Sound of Harris. At that juncture Alexander Gillies Ferguson, described as 'the veteran St Kilda tweed merchant', caught the overnight train from Glasgow to Kyle of Lochalsh and took the morning steamer from there to Tarbert in the hope of connecting with the *Hebrides* for her mercy mission. It was touch-and-go for a couple of days and when it seemed as if the *Hebrides* would not be able to make the hazardous journey; AG planned to hire a fishing boat at Leverburgh and relieve his son and nephew whose food supplies were virtually exhausted. On 30 August, however, a few days later than expected, the Hebrides headed out into the Atlantic and anchored in Village Bay at 9.10 p.m., just long enough to bring the two men off, while AG anxiously watched from the taffrail.

Seven years after the evacuation St Kilda hit the cinema screen. *Edge of the World* was the first major film made by Michael Powell and an outstanding turning-point in a career which, up to that time, had been devoted to B-features. Powell was captivated by the moving story of a community which had apparently given way to the forces of nature after a heroic struggle for existence lasting thousands of years. Naturally, he wished to make his film, a drama of the last days of the community centred on a Romeo and Juliet love story, on the actual location, and approached the Earl of Dumfries for permission to do so, but his lordship peremptorily refused. The Holbourn family, which owned Foula, remotest of the Shetland Isles and possessed of cliffs which were every bit as dramatic as St Kilda's, were much more amenable and, as a result, it gained considerable publicity when the seventy-five-minute film went on general release in 1937.

The names of the characters bore no resemblance to those of the St Kildans, nor, indeed, did the storyline have much bearing on reality, but the dramatic scenery and the powerful acting of John Laurie, Finlay Currie, Niall MacGinnis and others gave cinema audiences a pretty good impression of what life must have been like in the dying days of St Kilda. Incredibly, Alasdair Alpin MacGregor, author of the tedious and tendentious *Last Voyage to St Kilda*, sued Michael Powell for breach of copyright and tried to obtain an injunction to prevent the film's release, but he was quite literally laughed out of court. Powell himself later wrote a book entitled *20,000 Feet on Foula* (a reference to the film footage) which ranks as a classic on the art of film-making on a shoestring. *Edge of the World* was a tremendous success and has since acquired the status of a cult movie. In 2005 it was the centre-piece of the Edinburgh Film Festival, celebrating the centenary of Powell's birth, and it was screened along with *Britain's Loneliest Isle*, the documentary of 1923-29 which McCallum Orme had commissioned.

The spirit of St Kilda was kept alive not only by the efforts of Lord Dumfries but also of the islanders. In 1934 there was a Scottish Exhibition at Newcastle-upon-Tyne and Alexander Ferguson took one of the stands, the centrepiece of which was a genuine St Kilda loom at which Neil Gillies worked non-stop while his widowed mother, in her white mutch and shawl, knitted socks and gloves. The sides of the loom were plastered with the postcards which 'AG' continued to produce and which yielded a ready sale on and off the island. In 1938 Glasgow hosted the Empire Exhibition and in 'An Clachan', the re-creation of a typical Highland village, there was the typical St Kilda cottage (complete with thatched roof!). Finlay McQueen was now the oldest surviving male, his long white beard and shrew eyes creating a patriarchal impression beyond his years (he was actually seventy-five at the time). When King George VI and Queen Elizabeth toured the exhibition, Finlay was presented to them, and he even kissed the Queen's hand, just like the debutantes who 'came out' that year.

In the summer of 1938 the *Dunara Castle* and *Hebrides* between them made only four visits, between 16 May and 23 August. This was not for want of trying, for the *Dunara* had only been able to effect one landing out of the three trips she made. On 21 July she was in Tarbert, Harris, where Robert Atkinson and John Ainslie went aboard. They planned to spend several weeks on St Kilda, pursuing their lifelong ambition of charting the life cycle of that elusive bird, Leach's fork-tailed petrel, and then return to civilisation on the *Hebrides*. Atkinson would publish by far the best of all the books dealing with St Kilda. *Island Going* (Collins, 1949) devoted sixty-four pages to his sojourn on the island, providing the most poignant and evocative account of St Kilda ever written. Long out of print, this classic of island lore was reprinted in 1999 and has discovered a new readership, drawn largely from the vast army who have manned the working parties of the National Trust for Scotland since 1957.

This book contains the only account of what travelling on the *Dunara Castle* was really like. Most writers about St Kilda barely mentioned the vessel that got them there, and the various booklets published by Martin Orme, and latterly by McCallum Orme, indulged in purple prose that bore little relation to the grim truth. Atkinson was a good sailor who later explored the Hebrides in his own yacht, *Heather*, but Ainslie was the complete opposite, suffering the excruciating torments of sea-sickness in anything but a moderate swell. To compound his discomfort, the young men decided to travel steerage rather than enjoy the relative comfort of the saloon where the tourists congregated. Atkinson's description of their accommodation was graphic:

> The steerage quarters in the forepart of the ship measured two and a half paces by two and a half. We were the only occupants. The box was lined with shelves for sleeping on; ventilation was by the companion-way or hole leading up to the deck. There was a stove which we got going with cotton waste and soon regretted, as it filled the place with choking smoke and the portholes were bolted and painted shut.

They got under way at 3 a.m. the following day. At first the sea was so calm that 'a match flame burnt without a flicker' but once they were into the Minch and heading south towards the Sound of Harris the sea got up. When they sailed past Rodel, where they should have turned to starboard and entered the Sound, Atkinson was alarmed, then dismayed, when Captain Clark informed the passengers that St Kilda was out of the question and he was heading for Lochmaddy. His despondency was deepened by the lashing rain and the thick mist which reduced visibility to about 30m. All the rest of that rain-sodden gale-swept day the *Dunara* doggedly sailed southward, calling in at all the little ports to load or discharge cargoes which should have come after, not before, the excursion to St Kilda. Clark had commented at Lochmaddy that 'he might try for St Kilda from Barra, if the weather improved'. Atkinson's hopes were dampened by remarks of crew members that the *Dunara* had always worked St Kilda from the Sound of Harris; no one had ever heard of her going round Barra Head and then north-west into 70 miles of open Atlantic. At Castlebay, Ainslie decided that he had had enough. He left the ship there and headed homeward, taking the flight by Dragon Rapide biplane from the great cockle strand at the north of Barra to Renfrew.

One passage describes how the young ornithologist, who knew *With Nature and a Camera* by heart, assumed that the ship he was on was a descendant of the original *Dunara Castle* which had taken Richard and Cherry Kearton to St Kilda more than forty years earlier. Then he spotted the date on her brass bell, almost polished away – 1875: 'She was the self-same, identical *Dunara Castle*, here and now. I could not get over it. She was herself an Ancient Monument... This link by living ship was an abiding wonder and romance.'

Glasgow and West Highlands

CIRCULAR TOURS
(ABOUT SEVEN OR EIGHT DAYS)
TO THE
WESTERN ISLES

SEASON 1938

**The Steamers "HEBRIDES" and "DUNARA CASTLE"
are intended to sail as follows:—**

"HEBRIDES."	"DUNARA CASTLE."
April, - - - - - 11th and 21st	April, - - - 4th, 14th and 25th
May, - - - - 2nd, 12th and 23rd	May, - - - - 5th, 16th and 26th
June, - - - - 2nd, 13th and 23rd	June, - - - - 6th, 16th and 27th
July, - - - - 4th, 14th and 25th	July, - - - - 7th, 18th and 28th
August, - - - 4th, 15th and 25th	August, - - - 8th, 18th and 29th
September, - - 5th, 15th and 27th	September, - - 8th, 19th and 29th

EXTENDED CRUISES

ST. KILDA
"HEBRIDES"—2nd and 23rd June, 14th July and
4th August.

"DUNARA CASTLE"—16th May, 16th June, 18th July
and 18th August.

LOCH ROAG, LEWIS
"DUNARA CASTLE"—6th June (Special WHIT-WEEK CRUISE),
7th July, 8th August and 8th September.

ROUND THE ISLE OF SKYE
"HEBRIDES"—23rd May, 13th June, 4th and 25th July,
15th August and 5th September.

SKYE LOCHS AND IONA
"HEBRIDES"—25th August and 15th September.
"DUNARA CASTLE"—26th May, 27th June, 28th July,
29th August and 19th September.

Full particulars and berths booked on application to:—

McCALLUM, ORME & CO. LTD.
45 UNION STREET, GLASGOW, C.1

Telegraphic Address—McCallum, Glasgow   Telephone—Central 7126 (3 Lines)
(Private Branch Exchange)

Steamer handbill, 1938. The glossy brochures were aimed at the tourist trade, but these handbills provided the schedule of summer sailings.

The *Dunara Castle* at the dockside in Greenock, about 1926. Stores for some port on the West Highland coast are being hoisted on board, while passengers (including women) look on, prior to departure for a cruise to the Western Isles and 'Lone St Kilda'.

In fact, the skipper compromised and instead of steaming all the way south to Barra Head he took the shorter, though more treacherous, route through the Sound of Mingulay which probably cut an hour off the voyage. There was a heavy swell but at least the ocean was blue and not the horrible grey-green colour when the Atlantic is angry. The sun was setting around 10 p.m. that night when the *Dunara Castle* approached Hirta. The jagged cliffs, silhouetted against the fiery red sky, seemed like cardboard cut-outs but, as the ship drew nearer, Atkinson could appreciate the stupendous cliffs, the highest in the British Isles. The skipper was fearful of a change in the weather for the ship's boat was immediately lowered 'for one steerage derelict' and his eleven carefully labelled and numbered parcels. After a voyage that had lasted forty-eight hours instead of the customary seven, Atkinson landed just after midnight. At first he could make out nothing in the dark; no light was showing on the little jetty, but presently voices were heard in Gaelic or English and the young naturalist stepped ashore to be greeted by Neil Gillies whose first words were: 'What's the good of coming on a Sunday when we can't sell postcards?' But he did sell postcards and knitted socks, 'and thereby got into trouble with the cast-iron Sunday observances of Finlay MacQueen'. Atkinson dossed down in 'the House of Oiseval' for what remained of the night, in a room with straw palliasses on a proper bed.

The following day, Sunday 24 July, the weather was much more settled. The *Dunara Castle* still lay at anchor and presently disgorged her tourist passengers who spent the morning exploring the village while the three residents – Neil Gillies and his mother, and old Finlay McQueen – held a lengthy service in the little church. In the course of the morning Atkinson moved his belongings up from the old manse to the factor's house, and was just getting settled in on the ground floor when he was disconcerted to see some of the tourists peering through his window, though it seems that they were more embarrassed by the encounter than he was. Steeped in *With Nature and a Camera*, Atkinson was reliving the experiences of the Keartons who had occupied the self-same rooms forty-two years earlier. The passengers returned to the steamer in the early afternoon but the *Dunara* did not weigh anchor until the evening. Atkinson was sharing a *copa-té* with the Gillieses and old Finlay in cottage No.11 when the strident blast of the ship's whistle blew and they went out into the street to wave her goodbye. The *Dunara's* whistle was legendary in the West Highlands and Islands and quite unique in its sound, calculated to send every feathered being skyward.

During Atkinson's stay the Danish cruise liner *Esja* popped briefly into Village Bay, turned around and left almost as quickly without attempting a landing. Apparently this ship operated cruises round the Scottish islands from Glasgow every fortnight in the summer months and often touched at St Kilda, just long enough to allow passengers a glimpse of the desert isle. The Fishery Research Ship *Explorer* came in one day with her trawl down, marking the fish which were netted and then released. Fishermen who later caught one of these marked fish received a small reward for reporting where and when this happened and thus the movement of fish was scientifically charted. A party from the ship came ashore and from them Atkinson got news of Frank Fraser Darling and his family, who had set up a temporary home on the island of North Rona, which had been deserted since 1885 – apart from a brief stay by Atkinson and Ainslie in July–August 1936. The *Explorer* had been at Rona only four days previously.

The *Hebrides* arrived early on the morning of 9 August – 'a flat mazy calm and fresh dew-drenched dawn, opening to hot glare from a sky of unbroken lightest blue, hardly coloured' is how Atkinson described it. He and the three St

Kildans were packed and dressed, ready to depart, letting the island return to its abandoned state for the coming winter. Two boatloads of tourists came ashore and Neil did a brisk final trade in postcards, socks, gloves and scarves before bundling up the unsold stock and carrying it off until the following season. The ship sailed close to Boreray to let the tourists take photographs and then headed straight for the Sound of Harris. Apart from a brief halt at Rodel where Atkinson and his gear were dropped off on the local motor launch, the *Hebrides* sailed straight on without stopping until she reached Coll and Tiree. In due course, the purser's report by radiotelegram recorded in the *Glasgow Herald* that St Kilda had 'again been evacuated and left to the undisturbed possession of the seabirds'.

In the summer of 1939 the *Dunara Castle* called on 1 and 21 June, 22 July and 23 August, while the *Hebrides* visited St Kilda on 28 June, 20 July and 9 August. That summer McCallum Orme had produced a new handbill, with a picture of the *Hebrides* sailing past St Clement's Church, Rodel, at the eastern entrance to the Sound of Harris. The last trip of the *Dunara Castle* was dutifully recorded by the *Glasgow Herald*; no one could have realised, that day in August, that that would be the last visit of the McCallum Orme steamers to St Kilda.

The outbreak of the Second World War a week later severely curtailed the normal coastal traffic of the West Highlands and Islands. Both the *Dunara Castle* and the *Hebrides* continued with their regular service to the Western Isles, risking trips across the Minch despite the constant threat of German submarines. The aged *Dunara* survived the war but had a major mishap in March 1947 when she ran aground at Bunessan in Mull. She was stuck fast for about a week but eventually got afloat on a high spring tide without needing any help from the tug that had been standing by, and resumed her voyage as if nothing had happened. On 1 January 1948 McCallum, Orme & Co. Ltd became part of the MacBrayne group. This merger brought to an end the long and illustrious career of the *Dunara Castle*, and she made her final voyage to the West Highlands between 19 and 27 January that year. After that, she was laid up in the East India Harbour, Greenock, and eventually sold to Smith & Houston who had her towed to their breaker's yard at Port Glasgow the following summer. One of her boats was preserved and was on display in the 'St Kilda Explored' exhibition at Kelvingrove in 1996.

Although the *Dunara Castle* will forever be associated with St Kilda, it should be remembered that she was extremely popular at all the ports of call she served. She had especially close ties with the island of Colonsay. Captain Clark was a native of that island and his brother David owned the island hotel. Captain Clark was something of a poet and composed several ballads which alluded to the ship. A fine scale model of the *Dunara* may be seen in the museum at Campbeltown.

POPULAR SEA CRUISES
TO THE
WEST HIGHLANDS

A week's delightful sailing through the Outer Hebridean Islands, calling at Islay, Colonsay, Iona, Oban, Mull, Coll, Tiree, West of Skye, Harris, North and South Uist, and Barra,

TWICE EVERY TEN DAYS.

From Glasgow at **2·30** P.M., & from Greenock at **6·30** P.M., by the Steamers

"HEBRIDES" & "DUNARA CASTLE"

Fares from £9 to £10 5s., including Board.

ST. KILDA.

Nobody should fail to visit this lonely and romantic little spot in the Atlantic. Extended Cruises by "**Hebrides**" & "**Dunara Castle**" during Season—June till August.

Return Fare, including Board, £10.

LOCH ROAG.

Trips to this Loch, whose beauties are praised in Mr. Black's "Princess of Thule," are also made on Special Dates.

Return Fare, including Board, £10.

LOCH SCAVAIG, SKYE, for LOCH CORUISK.

Special Trips to this wild and beautiful Loch from which the famous Loch Coruisk can be visited. The scenery in this particular area is phenomenally majestic and grand. Nobody should fail to set foot on this wild and historic part of the Misty Isle of Skye.

Return Fare, including Board, £10.

ROUND THE ISLE OF SKYE.

CRUISES round this beautiful Island are made during the Summer Season and afford the Tourist a magnificent panoramic view of its wild mountainous scenery. A call is made at Mallaig on the mainland.

Return Fare, including Board, £10.

Note : Berth in four Berth Staterooms 2/6 extra. Two Berth Rooms & Deck Cabins 5/- extra

Full particulars, Tourist Programme, etc., free on application to

Telegraphic Address:
"McCALLUM, GLASGOW."
Telephone:
CENTRAL 7126 (3 Lines).

McCALLUM, ORME & CO., LTD.,
45 Union Street,
GLASGOW, C.1,

The steamer handbill of 1939, printed in blue and reducing the tour brochure to a single sheet which merely listed the St Kilda sailings with three words: 'June till August.' These were the very last sailings of the St Kilda steamers before the outbreak of the Second World War put an end to these excursions.

One of the jollyboats from the *Dunara Castle* has survived, and was on show at the 'St Kilda Explored' exhibition in the Museum and Art Galleries, Kelvingrove, Glasgow in 1996.

During the war the *Hebrides* was lent to MacBrayne and operated on their route between Oban and Tiree. While on this run she went aground near Coll but was successfully re-floated. This mishap seems ironic when one remembers that a high proportion of her crew were natives of Coll or Tiree. There is a well-known story concerning Captain John MacKinnon, a native of Coll, noted for his short temper. On one occasion, as the ship approached the treacherous coast of Arinagour, the island's tiny port, the mate, Donald MacFarlane (another Collach), telegraphed 'Slow Ahead' before being ordered by the captain. MacKinnon promptly ordered 'Full Ahead' and bawled at MacFarlane: 'Are you afraid of your own island?'

After the merger with MacBrayne, the *Hebrides* continued in service but purely as a cargo vessel. She continued to operate from Glasgow to Lochboisdale and Tarbert until 1952 when she was replaced by the *Loch Ard*. Like her old sister ship, she was laid up at Greenock before going to Smith & Houston's yard at Port Glasgow on 1 August 1955 and scrapped. Her brass bell was salvaged and for many years reposed in the lobby of the hotel in Tarbert, but when MacBrayne's launched their motor-vessel *Hebrides* in 1999 the bell was installed in the main passenger lounge, below a picture of her original namesake at her berth on the Broomielaw.

The story of St Kilda's subsequent history during the Second World War and its eventual re-occupation in 1957, first by the Royal Air Force and then the personnel of the Royal Artillery Range is fully covered in my book *Soldiering on St Kilda* (2002). When officials from the Ministry of Defence carried out a preliminary survey of the island in 1956 they were accompanied by several St Kildans, including Alexander Gillies Ferguson. Latterly, 'AG' had visited his old home aboard his own yacht, *Colonsay*, even during the war years – such was the incredible magnetic pull of the place.

Above: Model of the *Dunara Castle* in Campbeltown Museum, Argyll – a reminder that, although she is now chiefly remembered for her connection to St Kilda, this much-loved steamer was for many years a welcome sight in many other little ports round the coasts of the West Highlands.

Right: The brass ship's bell from the original SS *Hebrides*, now proudly displayed in the main lounge of her Caledonian-MacBrayne namesake.

In 1979 MacBrayne's celebrated their centenary and organised a cruise to the Western Isles aboard their flagship *Columba*, but as the heirs to McCallum Orme, MacBrayne included St Kilda in the itinerary. This visit was so successful that it was repeated the following summer. There the connection with the commercial steamship companies has come to an end. Today, St Kilda is the destination for approximately 1,500 to 2,000 visitors each year. Some come by private sailing boat or on the small motor cruisers chartered to take out the six working-parties organised by the National Trust for Scotland, to whom the Marquess of Bute bequeathed the islands in 1957. Others come on the cruise liners. Beginning with the MV *Meteor* in 1957 and continuing to the present day with the *Black Prince*, the National Trust has organised many cruises which usually include St Kilda – the jewel in the crown – in their itinerary; but many other ships, from the *Hebridean Princess* to the small motor vessels *Charna*, *Chalice*, and *Hjalmar Bjørge*, offer opportunities to visit St Kilda. And now there are even rigid inflatable boats (RIB) which operate from Leverburgh, Tarbert, and Loch Roag, and take the hardy to St Kilda in two hours, the Scottish equivalent of white-water rafting.

St Kilda today retains its magic. It is one of only twenty-three places worldwide to have *both* natural and cultural UNESCO World Heritage Status. In 2005 the seventy-fifth anniversary of the evacuation was marked by an exhibition in Edinburgh and a three-day conference in Lewis. On the actual anniversary, Patricia Ferguson (no relation of Neil and 'AG'), the Minister of Culture in the Scottish Parliament, flew in by helicopter to unveil a plaque recording the double UNESCO status. A few days earlier Norman Gillies, who had left the island as a boy of five in 1930, paid a last nostalgic visit to his birthplace to celebrate his eightieth birthday.

The concrete jetty erected more than a century ago is still going strong. The NTS working-parties have restored the feather store and though most of the houses are roofless ruins, the first six have been not just restored but equipped with running water and electricity. Although the military evacuated St Kilda in 1999 their impressive radar stations and other installations are maintained by a team of technicians employed by QinetiQ. There are regular flights to Benbecula by helicopter and St Kilda not only has all the benefits of modern telecommunications but even – a sign of the times – its own website.

Seeing all this, one cannot help speculating what might have been had the Government of 1930, and its various departments and agencies, not been so niggardly and short-sighted. The argument continues to rage over whether the removal of the human population might have been avoided. Sadly, it happened – and yet St Kilda lives, and flourishes as never before.

Index

Index